ACHIEVING SELF MASTERY

IN THE DIGITAL AGE

A GUIDE TO UNLIMITED EVOLUTION

MARCO D. MCKITHEN

About the Author

Marco D. McKithen is a highly decorated military veteran, advisor, and thought leader with over 17 years of success across corporate industries, which include healthcare, financial, and consulting services. His broad areas of expertise are leadership, team building, crisis management, operations, business development, process improvement, strategic planning, data analysis, marketing, finance, staffing, and organizing startup companies. He has successfully trained hundreds of individuals, including business managers, directors, and executives, and works across all demographics and generations.

Mr. McKithen has received multiple awards for exceptional military and corporate leadership. He is a Doctoral Candidate with a Master of Business Administration (MBA) in Complex Health Systems, a Bachelor of Science in Health Services Administration, and a certified Six Sigma Green Belt. He is passionate about teaching others and is an authorized adjunct professor of the business administration program at Highland Community College in Kansas State. Marco decided to become a writer to inspire and provide meaningful tools so others could become highly productive members of society. His experience comes from the perspective of those who face extreme adversity throughout life, and he aims to offer direct strategies and techniques to overcome it.

(The author's full bio is continued at the end of this book.)

Contents

Introduction   1

1. Situational Awareness   7

2. Exemplary Leadership   25

3. Limitless Capabilities   47

4. Living Without Fear   69

5. Mindset is Everything   91

6. Accountability, the Forgotten Skill   115

7. Support Systems   137

8. Time is of the Essence   163

9. Execute or be Executed   187

10. The Shield of Resilience   213

Conclusion   237

About The Author   241

Introduction

Today's world is filled with many distractions, and many people struggle with overcoming the challenge of focus and discipline. People are stuck with their heads down and eyes glued to their phone screens everywhere you look. The inventions of the Digital Age have drastically forced people to concentrate more on the lives of others than on themselves. What if I told you that global social media usage is trending upward at such a rapid rate that the average person's screen time now amounts to two and a half hours per day? What would you do with at least half of that time spent on personal growth and development? How much further ahead and accomplished would you be if you gave yourself an hour and fifteen minutes back daily? Well, many of you probably wouldn't even know what to do with yourselves. Let's admit it; you would likely spend the first thirty minutes getting in your way, stuck in your head, searching for an idea to spark, or trying to remember that million-dollar business plan that you just never wrote down. Or maybe you're like the younger version of me, fifteen years ago, searching for answers to get ahead and looking for that formula to become successful. No matter what you choose to do with an extra hour per day for self-development, at this moment, you will likely find yourself searching and seeking a clear path to greatness.

This is where this book fits in and why I wrote it. This book will give you the foundations of success; it is your personal development where it all begins.

If you made it this far, I commend you because you want more. I congratulate you because you are choosing a path to become extraordinary, improve yourself, stand out amongst your peers, and become the best version of yourself that you can be. I wrote this book for you, the former version of myself. Someone who in his mid-twenties knew that he had the drive to achieve success but had no direction and no guidance to get there. Whatever level you're at in life, you picked up the book because you want answers and value personal growth and development, or maybe you were just curious about what this title is all about. Whatever got you here, you're here, and these findings will open your mind to the true nature of personal development. They will give you a clear direction of what it takes and what you must do to become your best self.

What is Self–Mastery and Why it Matters

Merriam-Webster defined self-mastery as *the ability to control one's own desires or impulses.* This term dates back to the mid-16th century, and you will find thousands of references to it across the internet. While Merriam-Webster's definition is concise, it does not embody the full magnitude of what self-mastery truly is. Therefore, I define self-mastery as *the overcoming of oneself and the ability to obtain complete control of one's thoughts, actions, and outcomes.* Achieving it allows one to translate their spiritual, intellectual, and emotional states into the physical realm. Many people would relate this concept to the universal law of attraction, or *The Secret,* as described by author Rhonda Byrne. However, those concepts argue that consistent positive thinking will eventually manifest into reality, and that is not the case. Positive thinking alone will not get you anywhere without action and intentional effort. This is why the pursuit of self-mastery is so vital. It goes beyond thinking, and this book will help you identify what actionable steps to take to push yourself beyond your current limits to a new level that you only dreamed possible.

As we wrap up this introduction, I want you to do a quick exercise to put things into perspective. Consider the examples of the most highly successful people you admire today and ask yourself these questions. Are they alone, without a team, without someone or something to lead? What do they attribute to their achievements and continued success? When did their lives change, and how do they consistently perform at such high levels? Many of these answers will point to discipline, rituals, routine habits, consistency, goal-setting, clear thoughts, etc. What you will come to realize is that they have actually achieved or are in the pursuit of self-mastery. Successful people win because they don't just think differently; they act differently. They put in the time to learn themselves so that they can react better to stressful situations. One cannot successfully command and lead others until one understands how to lead oneself. As these individuals continue to climb the ladder, the level of responsibility and stress increases. Therefore, personal strengths become even more valuable, and weaknesses are exposed. If you cannot gain control over your own thoughts, emotions, and actions, you cannot expect to lead others and teach them how to become great genuinely.

In this Digital Age, distractions are at an all-time high, and time is the most valuable asset. If you want to learn how to mitigate these distractions and develop the skills to live up to your full potential, then the pursuit of self-mastery is the key, and *Achieving SELF-MASTERY in the Digital Age* will allow you to open new doors. I have achieved many personal accolades, overcome adversity, broken numerous barriers, developed and led multiple successful organizations, and achieved educational success at the doctorate level. Many will also speak about my determination, grit, and discipline and wonder how I continue to raise the bar while remaining calm and approachable. Well, this was all by design, and this book will describe my formula for true self-development and personal growth. You will learn about ten attributes that are easy to understand and apply. Here are the Ten Pillars of Self-Mastery.

Situational, Exemplary, Limitless, Fearless, Mindful, Accountable, Supporting, Timely, Executor, Resilient

SELF-MASTER

Now, without further delay, here is how you achieve self-mastery in the digital age!

1

Situational Awareness

The Bigger Pot Theory

Why do plants stop growing in small pots? Container size relevant to plant growth has been a burning research topic for decades. Biologists, scientists, and researchers worldwide have conducted significant experiments to understand this correlation between them. In most cases, these studies produced considerable evidence that doubling a plant's container size led to more than a forty percent increase in the plant's size. So, what causes this stunted size increase, and why would simply providing a bigger pot lead to such significant growth? The reason plants outgrow their containers is because their roots outgrow the soil. Plant soil provides essential nutrients that are absorbed through its roots. Thus, when the roots can no longer expand, the plant forces itself to stop growing as a response to preserving its life. Hence, the plant doesn't die; it just stops growing to keep the soil-to-root ratio at a point where it will not destroy its nutritional source. Clever right? This natural response to stop growing is the plant's form of situational awareness. Henceforth, when the owner offers a bigger pot, they allow the plant to grow because it can now flourish by expanding its roots in the additional soil, which holds all its resources.

The bigger pot theory is relevant to human growth and development because, like plants, we also stop growing if our environment is not conducive to allowing it. This reasoning is why you see many people settle and become complacent. It is why people give up on life and live averagely by facing a reality they cannot grow past. They are not trying to understand their situation and how their environment impacts them, or maybe they are so stuck in it that they would stop growing to avoid discomfort. This is a sad reality but true in so many cases. Can you think of anyone who fits this description? Merriam-Webster defined the term "situation" as a *position with respect to conditions and circumstances,* while "awareness" is *knowledge and understanding that something is happening or exists.* Thus, "situational awareness" is *understanding how one's current conditions and circumstances impact their position.* Just as the plant realizes it can still live as long as its soil is cared for, it also relies on the owner to provide a bigger pot to help it grow beyond its environment. Therefore, as individuals seeking growth and development, you must first understand your circumstances to assess the need for a bigger pot. This is the first step in self-mastery.

Facing Reality

One of the most critical aspects of situational awareness is facing reality. The internet is filled with people displaying their glamorous lifestyles, and it is so saturated that individuals tend to believe that social media is reality. Some people often live through others' perspectives so much that it adversely impacts their own dreams. It is easy to get hypnotized and think that the things you see are well beyond your reach. They are attainable; however, you rarely see the effort and struggles many of these people went through to achieve their success. The pursuit of self-mastery is a guiding light to help you get there, but you must first take a step back and look at yourself in the mirror. You must identify and analyze the barriers preventing you from reaching beyond your current reality. Are you at a point where you feel you are hitting a brick wall in your career, finances, or personal development? Do you want to reach a position with unlimited growth potential in all areas? If so, understanding your situation will be a key to unlocking this path because all conditions are unique to each individual. The following story will help deepen your understanding of this concept and allow you to grasp the connection between reality and situational awareness.

A little over a decade ago, I started this journey

of self-mastery. At the time, I didn't know what I was embarking upon; I just knew I was unhappy and wanted more out of life. The only thing I had going for me was this desperate hunger for success, and my work ethic was abnormal. However, my finances were severely unstable; I had been through numerous home evictions, struggled to pay bills, and had a family to tend to. My environment contributed to my downfall, but I opened my eyes before reaching my breaking point. The city I grew up in had few examples of successful people I could relate to. Nonetheless, I did not use this as an excuse. Instead, I found myself reading self-help books to expand my mind, watching documentaries, and trying to understand the lifestyles of the successful and wealthy. I then realized a common thread: "These people all have similar fundamental characteristics." I thought to myself.

This awakening forced me to face my reality and analyze my situation. Many people faced with similar situations embrace the victim mentality. They fall into this trap where they believe no one wants to see them prevail. You'll hear them say things like, "The system isn't built for people like me." Or, "I'm not working for those types of people." Sound familiar? These negative thoughts and statements create hatred towards others when the actual issue lies in the individual's lack of situational awareness. My relentless search for more allowed me to face reality, and just like the plant does, as described earlier, I discovered that I needed a bigger pot of soil to expand my roots. My culture did not prepare me to get to the level I dreamed of. Facing reality during that time helped me develop a path by identifying how society viewed me. I was a young, uneducated minority with dreams, and I began to embrace it!

As previously stated, embracing my reality helped me identify my actual societal position. Honestly, my goals did not align with my surroundings, and I quickly knew I needed to make drastic changes. The first change was accepting that I needed to pursue higher education. Not everyone needs to attend college, but I grew to understand that I would need to learn how to hold intelligent conversations and build relationships with like-minded people to reach my ideal success level. The people around me could not teach me those things; I realized that and found the best avenue for me to gain those skills. However, your situation may look much different than mine. Thinking at this height of awareness also made me conscious of people's negative perceptions of me because of my physical appearance. Therefore, I focused on improving my posture, grooming standards, and presentation. I even started wearing suits and dressing differently. I quickly learned I needed to take myself seriously before expecting anyone else to take me seriously. At that defining moment, I realized that I had the power to control and shape my own destiny.

Psychological Geography

You may be thinking, "What does geography have to do with situational awareness?" This is a valid question, and back when I first began analyzing my situation, I understood things much better by simplifying them. So, let's imagine this scenario—You scratch off a lottery ticket that reads, *"You win,"* except instead of showing you what you won, the card states that *"all winners must call this phone number to claim their prize."* You are excited, jumping for joy, and tell your significant other you are a winner. Now, you are joyful but anxious about calling the number. However, you dial it anyway. The phone number then leads you to a recording telling you to punch in your winning ticket number to hear what you have won. You and your partner's palms are sweaty at this point, but you continue. The recording then announces your prize. It states, *"You have won a month-long lifetime trip to paradise, useable annually. This trip is filled with beautiful beaches, free food, and drinks; you will stay in a five-star hotel with all the possible recreation. You must only know that this trip is on a remote island, and you must provide your own transportation."* After accepting this news, what is the first thing you will do? Most people will try to discover where the destination is and then figure out a plan to get there. Our brains are naturally wired this way, but people don't apply the same thinking to their goals for some reason. Goals can actually be approached as geographical destinations psychologically. You simply need to determine your location and distance from the goal, just as you would in this winning trip to paradise example. This simple geography concept will help you to:

1. Identify your goals (the destination)
2. Analyze where you physically are (your location)
3. Develop your path (transportation)

I gave you this example so you could genuinely understand the simplicity of situational awareness. The key is this—One must first identify their current position before getting to their destination. Doing the opposite will cause extreme confusion, frustration, and loss of time. Not fully understanding where you are in life will literally end up getting you lost. And if you've ever been physically lost, you know it's a painful feeling you want to avoid at all costs.

Why People Try Avoiding Their Situations

Most people are unwilling to face their situations because of denial. They would rather trick themselves into thinking that things are going better than they genuinely are to avoid the feeling of disappointment. Living in denial is much easier to handle than reality because facing reality forces change, and change is scary for many individuals. Think about this question: Have you ever dreaded taking your car to the dealership for general maintenance because *you know* the mechanic will find something else that requires repair or replacement? Of course, you've been there; we all have. Those conversations are usually awkward; some people avoid the dealership or hire a personal mechanic to keep their vehicle running just enough to get them around. However, what the dealership mechanics are offering is the ability to allow your vehicle to perform at its maximum level. This scenario describes the same concept that applies to your personal denial of reality. Our natural tendency is to adapt and evolve. Hence, as described in this example, your mind naturally wants you to perform at your maximum level.

As I mentioned, living in denial is more convenient than accepting change. Having someone tell you that you need to change is easy to brush off because you can just switch the topic or stop talking to them altogether. However, telling yourself that you need to change is a much more challenging conversation to have. The thought lingers in your mind until you actually do something about it. So, instead, people become dishonest with themselves to believe they are doing the best they can with the skills and resources their higher power gave them. This is a false reality; if it describes you, you must wake up and stop lying to yourself! When people live in denial, they either lack the confidence to improve, feel like they don't have the support to do better, or fear the embarrassment of looking like they don't have things under control. They simply don't believe they can change or are just too arrogant to admit their flaws. Being too prideful is the path of destruction. Denial won't get you anywhere except for where you are now. It will not allow you to reach beyond your ceiling. Therefore, you shouldn't let these foolish reasons prevent you from becoming your true self.

Another reason people tend to avoid facing their situations is that they are lazy. As discussed, denial helps you avoid change. You may require substantial change depending on how far you are from your goals, where you are in life, and your career. The one thing identifying your current situation will do is expose the level of personal change required. This is great for those who love a challenge, but for others, the idea might be less exciting. Therefore, people either reduce their goals or stay content because evolution involves work, and many don't want to do extra work. When you discover

'Living in denial
is much easier to
handle than reality
because facing
reality forces
change, and change
is scary for many
individuals.'

your position in life relative to your goals, improving it requires commitment. Vince Lombardi once said, *"The quality of a person's life is in direct proportion to their commitment to excellence, regardless of their chosen field of endeavor."* Understandably, we only have a limited time on this earth (which I will discuss in Chapter 8). Wouldn't you rather live a high-quality life instead of one that is subpar? If so, the faster you can identify your reality, the quicker you can begin developing yourself to start achieving your goals. Being lazy is far too common, and you can actually outperform your competition by proactively improving yourself.

How to Practice Situational Awareness

As you previously learned, practicing situational awareness is vital to your growth and development. These Ten pillars of Self-Mastery are not followed in a particular order. However, it is best to practice situational awareness first because it serves as your foundation for unlocking self-mastery. It is the grounding principle toward achieving your goals. As you've learned, you can only reach your destination once you know where you currently are. Thus, practicing and gaining situational awareness will prepare you to take on the other nine pillars of self-mastery. It is critical to note that practicing situational awareness is a continuous application required at every barrier you reach to help you get to your next level. Skipping this step will only set you back because you must always identify your reality. Now, let's look at ways to conquer this vital attribute in the Digital Age.

1. **Write down your goals**

   a. Writing down your goals will allow you to apply more than thought to what you want to achieve. The action of writing things down will allow your mind to accept it as an objective. These goals will become focal points written in history, but if they are not logged somewhere, they will not exist. Where the mind goes, the body will follow.

b. As described in the psychological geography section, your path is determined by your current position relative to your destination. Think big, and don't worry about the course at this time; that will come as you move along the rest of this book and unlock the other pillars of self-mastery.

2. Use online tools to conduct research

a. You can conduct primary research online to discover the requirements for specific careers, resources, skills, associations, and other vital needs to reach specific goals. This type of search can also help you explore other goals and find the ones you are most excited about.

b. Using online search engines can help you learn more about your demographics to understand your surroundings better. You can discover if there are better areas that are more supportive of your growth by researching historical data.

3. Follow your mentors online

a. Follow your mentors on social media to learn more about their backgrounds and lifestyles. You can explore their surroundings, learn about their motivational factors, and tap into their community. This approach will also allow you to network with others who may be on a similar path as you.

b. Communicating with your mentors by engaging in their posts can open doors for you. These mentors may be approachable people who would love to help someone like you learn more, or they can share resources to help you grow. Make sure you are always coming from a place of humility and thanks.

4. Be truthful to yourself

a. The best thing you can do to evolve is to be honest with yourself. Don't let social media influence you to become a liar to your followers and supporters. Learn to use social media as a tool to help you instead of a platform for false narratives.

b. Don't compare yourself with others in a negative way. If you are the type that compares yourself with others on social media, approach it by trying to learn what they are doing that you are not. Handle comparisons by being honest and uncovering your shortcomings, but be sure only to analyze the person's skills and attributes because your starting point may differ.

5. Take your situation for what it is worth

a. Realize that you have the power to overcome

your situation. Take it for what it is worth and focus on changing it. Don't dwell in the past; look toward your future by pursuing self-mastery. Who you were yesterday does not have to define who you will become tomorrow.

b. Understand that others have been in similar situations as you, or worse, depending on where you are in life. Embrace learning as much as possible about your circumstance to develop a plan to overcome it.

Practicing situational awareness will define your evolution. Ignoring this step will not help you reach your full potential or get close to your highest success level. As I mentioned, this will be a painful process for many people. However, I shared these examples with you to help you understand how crucial it is to embrace your reality. You can start to shape your path once you get past the denial, pridefulness, laziness, or whatever prevents you from analyzing your situation. By applying these approaches, you will already be at an advantage. This formula will give you a baseline to begin your personal growth journey. It will allow you to continue climbing the ladder as you assess your situation at each barrier you experience. The more you embrace situational awareness, the more it becomes habitual and allows you to grow exponentially. As you move throughout this book and learn more about becoming a self-master, you will continuously reveal reminders about situational awareness and see why it is always relevant to your success.

2

Exemplary Leadership

Jumping off a Bridge

As a child, I always remembered my mother asking me, "So if Johnny jumps off a bridge, are you going to jump off a bridge too?" I'm sure you've been asked that question once or twice in your lifetime. I can recall countless times being asked some form of that question. Ironically, as a parent, I often discover myself asking my children the same thing. I always knew this was a trick question. So why do parents waste their breath asking it, knowing the child will never answer and say, "Yes, of course?" First, let's try to understand the thought behind it and what triggered the question in the first place. Parents primarily ask it because they learn their child is hanging with someone who is a bad influence. This individual usually has negative qualities, has done something to ruin the parent's trust, or has actively engaged in hostile activity with the parent's child. Therefore, the question gets asked because the parent does not want their child to follow in Johnny's footsteps. Now, what if Johnny was the opposite? What if they were a standup child who went above and beyond in everything they did, received straight A's in school, stayed out of trouble, was well-mannered and athletic, and kept their home spotless without being asked? In this case, I'm sure most parents would want their children to interact and learn from this extraordinary kid! I am absolutely sure I would.

I provided this example to put this next self-mastery pillar into proper perspective. The Johnny jumping off a bridge question is a figure of speech and basic concept describing influence and leadership. People either have a positive, neutral, or negative effect on your life; it is the same for your impact on others. Seeking the path of success and pursuing self-mastery requires ensuring that the impact that others have on you and that you have on others is always positive. When either party negatively influences the other, it can hinder one's success or cause a downward spiral that will take tremendous effort or time to overcome. Conversely, when the parties positively influence one another, they form a leader-and-follower bond, with both pushing each other toward greatness. This is why the attribute of "exemplary" is required to achieve self-mastery. It is also why many people seek apprenticeships, mentors, and life coaches. Exemplary leaders are followed because of their expertise and because they can teach others how to achieve the same success.

The notion of leading by example is a powerful approach to all involved in the process. Even so, teams led by exemplary leaders can overcome unthinkable obstacles and frequently achieve whatever they set their sights on. Merrian-Webster defines "exemplary" as *someone deserving imitation because of excellence* and *someone serving as an example, instance, or illustration.* Therefore, "exemplary leadership" describes *someone who has achieved greatness in their field and leads by the example others want to emulate.* These exemplary leaders are so influential that their followers are willing to jump off a bridge because they trust in the leaders' path. They are successful because they know their strengths and trust their instincts. When sacrifices are necessary, they jump off the bridge first, then scan the horizon for threats and barriers when they land before allowing their team to take damage. This is the type of leader you want to become, and you will learn the fundamentals of getting there throughout this chapter.

Leader versus Boss

Most people refer to the terms leader and boss interchangeably. Depending on who you are speaking with, you will typically hear misuses of both words. I cannot make this any more precise—a leader and a boss are not the same. Simply stated, leaders lead, and bosses dictate! Leaders are those you hear about that improve the lives of those around them. They are willing to do whatever it takes to progress their teams, even getting in the trenches and getting their hands dirty. Leaders don't expect their followers to do the things they would not or have not done themselves. They are supportive, provide resources, and consistently think as a team. On the other hand, bosses give commands and will not go out of their way to support their team. They think of personal gain at the expense of others. Frequently, bosses set unrealistic expectations of their teams and provide just enough support to get the job done. However, there are good, successful bosses who accomplish substantial goals, but those accomplishments typically do not benefit the team members. Whereas, when good, successful leaders accomplish substantial goals, those accomplishments benefit the entire group and usually correlate with the individual growth of the team members.

There are also significant misunderstandings of organizational and corporate titles. Even if someone gains a specific title, like supervisor, manager, director, executive, etc., it does not make them a leader. These titles allow the individual to gain the term boss because they assume a position of authority, but becoming a true leader occurs over time. Leaders must prove themselves through their team or group efforts. Unlike bosses, they also do not have to be authoritative figures. This is a critical point to note because of how commonly people misuse the terms. You will see many examples of leaders who may have yet to receive an authoritative title. However, they are leaders because of their positive influence on others and dedication to developing themselves to support their followers. Eventually, whether they have a position of authority or not, in due time, they will assume the role or title that aligns with their leadership efforts because they attract greatness and positivity. There are typically three levels of leadership: good, great, and exemplary. However, not all leaders reach exemplary levels, which you will learn more about as you continue to read on.

Now that you understand the main differences between a boss and a leader, I want to ask you a few questions. What type of figure are you today? Are you a boss or a leader? Would you follow yourself if your life depended on it? Be honest and think deeply before answering those questions. You want to become the type of leader that you are willing to die for. Followers of exemplary leaders take the teachings of their leaders as gospel. They know their leader will give them the best advice and set the best path for them to follow because the leader has gone through it themselves and lives to tell the tale. They genuinely lead by the example they set, and you will soon learn how to develop these traits.

Become the Change you Want to See

"Men make history and not the other way around. In periods where there is no leadership, society stands still. Progress occurs when courageous, skillful leaders seize the opportunity to change things for the better."— Harry S. Truman, former US President.

Now, even more than ever, social media has provided a sounding board for the complainers. This population of people greatly outweighs the change agents. You know who these individuals are: those who complain about everything wrong with society but won't dare to do anything about it. They will blame their family, the Congressmen, the schools, law enforcement, the military, Uncle Sam, and practically anyone they can point their fingers at. But you know who they won't blame for their misfortunes? You guessed it—themselves! For some reason, the complainers will whine and talk about what everyone else is not doing to improve society but won't put the same energy into improving it themselves. Sure, avoiding looking in the mirror and convincing yourself that one person will not change anything is easy. Many people get caught up in that way of thinking and spend their entire lives blaming others for their lack of success or harsh circumstances. But as you learned in the previous chapter, facing reality is demanding but critical to change, and avoiding it is a sure way to keep the status quo. Therefore, if you genuinely want to experience change, *you* must become the change *you* want to see.

Becoming the change you want to see means that you must dedicate your life to becoming the one thing that upsets you the most. Here are some examples to help you better understand this concept. —*If you hate how things are in your community, become a politician or local representative. If you hate that minorities have poorer health outcomes than other groups, become a healthcare worker or professional. If you hate that racial biases still exist in law enforcement, education, and other systems, become a lawyer, law enforcement officer, or educational professional. If you hate that your family historically has financial issues, become a banker or public accountant.* — I am sure you now get the point. Becoming the change you want to see requires identifying what you do not like about society and then focusing on changing it by taking steps to become influential. It is about representation and playing your part in the community by becoming a change agent instead of a complainer. Change agents are people who dedicate their lives to having a positive impact on the world. They are the ones you hear about in global history or learn about through your family lineage as the people who built legacies for generations. They are the heroes and exemplary leaders who decided to be great and change lives. Would you consider yourself a change agent? What have you done to become the change you want to see? In the following example, I'll share what has worked for me and why

'Becoming the change you want to see requires identifying what you do not like about society and then focusing on changing it by taking steps to become influential.'

others refer to me as a change agent and exemplary leader.

You learned a little about my background in the previous chapter, and as I mentioned, I grew up with few mentors and role models; my mother was one of them. She was a brave woman who taught me to be relentless, focused, and limitless. Her teachings taught me that I could do anything I set my mind to, and she helped me learn about situational awareness. Around the time I started facing my reality and applying situational awareness, I made a life-changing decision to become a positive example. I realized that too many people faced similar situations as me and grew to learn that many of them needed a genuine leader even though they didn't admit it. Therefore, I started this course of becoming the change, which continues to drive my success today. I dedicated my life to becoming an exemplary leader for my family and community. I chose to become the one to create change by striving to do what many around me believed was impossible.

I had every opportunity to give up and every excuse to become a failure, another statistic. I faced extreme poverty, homelessness, violence, crime, racism, legal issues, lawsuits, and numerous near-death experiences. Still, I did not let those obstacles define me. Instead, I faced them head-on, learning from every experience and gaining the knowledge to overcome and mitigate them. My family historically faced a similar continuous cycle of obstacles, so I became obsessed with breaking it. This obsession led me down a path of becoming wildly successful, accomplishing many of my generation's firsts. I became the first to serve in the military, receiving numerous awards and medals. I am my family's first to obtain a graduate degree, graduating with honors at the top of my class. I am the first to enter doctoral school, completing the first year with a perfect 4.0 GPA. I became the first to start and lead multiple businesses and serve in numerous corporate leadership roles, breaking systematic racial barriers along the way. As a result, my children have massive goals that I can support and provide the resources to achieve them. However, I don't share this information to brag but to show you the true power of exemplary leadership. My obsession with setting an example allows me to continue to beat the odds. It allows me to become a mentor to others who seek help. I didn't complain about not having people to show me the way, but instead, I became a change agent to give others hope around me. When you focus on becoming the change as I did, you can break any barriers and vicious cycles you may face. Your dedication to this will allow you to improve the lives of others, and you will see that one person can create significant change. As a result, personal success will become a byproduct of becoming the change you want to see.

Why People Struggle to Become Exemplary Leaders

Being an exemplary leader takes work to accomplish and deliberate action. As you learned, reaching this level takes a specific type of person. Exemplary leadership is a life-long commitment that requires pushing yourself and others. Leaders struggle to achieve this level mainly because they haven't pushed themselves hard enough to move others with the same force. Leading is terrific, but when you do not hold your own feet to the fire, you will not expect the same from your followers. Thus, leaders fall short of exemplary because they lead but take it easy on everyone. They tend to take a passive approach, just setting a good example, but not a relentless one. To become an exemplary leader, you must be aggressive in your attack. Leaders find this challenging because they are just too soft! Now, I am not telling you to become an authoritarian, but you must set high expectations for yourself so that you can demand the same from others. Do you find it difficult to push your followers? If so, you may not be pushing yourself hard enough. Or do you see yourself pushing so hard that they get frustrated or unmotivated? If this describes you, you are likely setting unrealistic expectations that you would not do or have not done yourself. This leads me to another reason why people struggle to become exemplary leaders.

As many leaders climb the ladder, they develop this sense of entitlement and believe they are above putting in the legwork to get the job done. I have met thousands of leaders and worked alongside hundreds, and in my experience, this belief has become a commonality. Leaders should always work to their highest level to maximize output and delegate as much as possible, but there are times when getting in the trenches is required. Imagine this: You are starting a new company or trying to expand your current one and need a specific role to be filled. Your current staff cannot take on any more tasks without other things falling behind. You realize that recruiting the highly needed position will take time, but taking time will slow down potential profits. However, you have the skill set to handle the task yourself. What would you do next? Many leaders would continue recruiting while keeping things as they currently are. Others would split the workload amongst the current group until they fill the position, at the cost of reducing progress in other areas. A few leaders would jump in and do the job themselves. However, exemplary leaders would recruit, split the workload, and jump in to do the job themselves! They would put in the extra effort in all areas to move things along. As a leader, you should never feel above getting your hands dirty and putting in the work. That mentality will slow down your progress, but it is widespread. I sometimes prefer and look for opportunities to get in the trenches because it has many benefits. It will allow you to keep your skills sharp and your team motivated. It will also eliminate excuses for lack of performance from your followers and help you identify areas that require better processes since you will perform the same tasks. You can manage more effectively and maximize efficiency.

The third common reason people don't become exemplary leaders is because they lack confidence. As mentioned earlier in this chapter, exemplary leaders are successful because they know their strengths and trust their instincts. Besides their impact on their followers, the key differentiator is their ability to make sound decisions under pressure. Hence, trust is a critical component of exemplary leadership; followers trust their leaders to make the best decisions. You must understand that you need to develop high levels of self-confidence and trust your gut when put to the test. When leaders lack confidence, they do not fully trust themselves. You cannot expect others to trust you if you don't even trust yourself. Therefore, lacking confidence as a leader can become a virus that will contaminate your team. However, don't confuse confidence with arrogance because there is a clear difference. I like to think of these two in the sense of force and direction. Arrogance is a weakness that causes one to push and look down upon another, while confidence is a strength that allows one to move forward and pull up an individual. Pursuing self-mastery will teach you more about building confidence and becoming fearless. As you continue to read on, Chapter 4 will explain how to develop this crucial attribute. For now, it is wise to wrap your head around these common reasons leaders fail to reach exemplary levels so you don't fall victim to these issues.

How to Become an Exemplary Leader

Early leadership studies began in the late 19th century with the introduction of the Great Man Theory by Thomas Carlyle. The Great Man Theory suggested that leaders were born and not developed. This theory was later opposed as researchers began understanding that leadership could be taught through learned behavior. Over time, numerous styles emerged as people noticed that leadership comprises specialized traits, attitudes, skills, and behaviors, also known as characteristics. With new concepts like charismatic, transactional, transformational, and servant leadership, many individuals need help identifying a clear superior leadership style. Each of these styles I mentioned has specific weaknesses that, when exploited, render the type ineffective. This is where exemplary leadership comes in and why it is so effective.

The exemplary leadership style embodies most of these styles' blended positive characteristics. However, it replaces the weaknesses of each with the strengths of the others. For example, servant leaders typically lose authority when faced with a follower who bends the rules. Their manner is more caring, which poses challenges for disciplinary action and accountability. In comparison, exemplary leaders' aggressive nature and clear expectations allow them to discipline when necessary and hold themselves and others highly accountable, embodying the transactional style. I also mentioned the significance of confidence in exemplary leadership and how it helps instill trust; this aligns with the charismatic leadership style. Last, you learned how exemplary leaders shape the lives of those around them by becoming the change. This characteristic aligns with transformational leadership. Therefore, exemplary leadership is superior because it merges the highest strengths of today's most impactful leadership styles. Would you like to learn more about becoming an exemplary leader? Let's look at some things that have worked for me and some steps you can take to achieve it.

1. **Take a personality assessment**

    a. In the previous chapter, you learned the power of situational awareness and why it is crucial to achieving self-mastery. As you make yourself aware of your circumstances, it is also beneficial to learn about yourself. You must understand your current leadership style and how you react to specific situations. Many personality assessments are accessible online and will help you discover your style. Some of my favorite assessments are the Myers-Briggs Type Indicator® and 16Personalities.

    b. Uncovering your current leadership style will

allow you to understand your thoughts and discover your strengths to know what you're up against. Once you learn where you stand, you will know how far you are from gaining exemplary leadership characteristics. You can then begin working on yourself to become a more effective leader and maximize your potential.

2. **Invest in learning about your team members**

   a. Take the time to learn about your team members. Your team members can be your direct reports, students, athletes, family, and anyone you manage or lead directly. Spend one-on-one time with them and schedule routine meetings to build better relationships. This action will help you understand what motivates them and how you can help your followers develop themselves. Exemplary leaders care about the well-being of their team members.

   b. The most successful leaders focus on the strengths of their team members and use them to their full potential. Learning about your team members will also allow you to discover their strengths. Followers are more engaged in the team when their leader pushes them to use their strengths instead of trying to build up their weaknesses. Many leaders have this completely wrong, but now you know better. Your team members will appreciate you for taking these steps.

3. **Commit to become a change agent**

   a. You need to commit to becoming a change agent. When browsing social media and hearing current news, consider the negative issues that trigger you. If there is something that you stand for and want to see changed, start asking yourself what you can do to contribute to making a difference. Don't get caught up in the mindset that one person cannot create positive change. Creating social change requires individuals who are committed to common goals.

   b. Start small and then go big by creating positive social change within your home, workplace, or community. Depending on where you are, your journey may be long, and there may be many levels you will need to achieve to reach your end goal of the change you want to see. Hence, creating small changes first will allow you to break down the goal into multiple levels and show you how possible social change is when you are committed. You can celebrate your small wins as you work toward your long-term goals.

4. **Set high expectations for yourself**

   a. You must demand more of yourself to demand more of others. When you hold yourself to higher standards, you will achieve more. Exemplary leaders set lofty goals and continue stretching themselves. When followers see their leader reaching their goals and raising the bar, they will follow suit or eventually be replaced. This approach will allow you to develop a successful team that continues growing and reaching its goals.

b. Remember you are striving for self-mastery, the highest level you can achieve. Becoming the type of leader who is a high achiever will produce similar results. Massive levels of success proportionately correlate to massive goals. The opposite is also true. Don't sell yourself short and settle for less than greatness.

5. Invest in continuing education

a. Never believe that you know everything or that it is too late to educate yourself. Your followers will respect your knowledge and challenge you at times. Investing in continuing education will allow you to remain sharp in your industry and personal development. Over time, your knowledge will become outdated. Thus, your growth will rely on your ability to continue your journey. Exemplary leaders are devoted to keeping up with the times and staying relevant.

b. Search for online courses, programs, or

associations to help you continue your educational journey. Even if you do not possess a degree, you can obtain certifications or knowledge that will help you grow. Your clients, colleagues, and followers will all appreciate this and respect you even more. This step produces endless dividends.

This chapter taught you that leading others is vital to your success. However, you can't expect people to follow you because of your title or position in life. They will follow you because you do what others are afraid of and show them the way. Becoming an exemplary leader is mandatory for achieving self-mastery because it will allow you to gain the characteristics to lead others as you would lead yourself. The concepts and suggestions I discussed will help you become the leader you need to be to achieve high results. Exemplary leadership is more than just leading by example; it is about continuous personal growth and achievement that gets taught to the team members. It is about developing an extraordinary team, improving the lives of your followers, and improving society. Exemplary leaders make everything around them better and lead highly successful lives. They create legacies and live on through the lives they directly impact. Some would even suggest they achieve immortality because of their quest to make a difference. Nothing is impossible for these types of leaders.

3

Limitless Capabilities

The Marathoner

With all things equal, what causes one person to go further in life than the other? Before answering this question, I want to share a popular concept with you that is not usually described in full detail. I'm sure you've heard some variation of the phrase, "Life is a marathon, not a sprint." Of course, you've heard it. We all have, but what does this saying actually mean? First, let's explore what's involved in running a single marathon and its history.

A marathon is just beyond 26 miles or 42 kilometers. If you've ever run one mile, you know this distance is highly intimidating. People usually don't just wake up one day and decide to run a marathon. It requires strict discipline and training. Marathoners train for up to 20 weeks, running hundreds of miles before completing their final marathon run. Successful completion takes an average of four and a half hours but can last up to 8 hours for some. In comparison, sprinting is most commonly judged by the 100-meter dash and takes an average of 14 seconds, with record holders aiming for less than 10 seconds. Sprinters also undergo strict training; however, sprinting is about speed, not distance. Marathoners train to avoid injury and fatigue, as the journey can take a toll on one's body and cause severe problems and health risks. Now, I'm not trying to downplay sprinting, but many people can complete a sprint. I can't say the same for completing a marathon because they're rigorous, and the human body is not naturally prepared to engage in one. Here's something to consider: The original marathoner, Phillippides, was a Greek messenger who died after running a 25-mile stretch from the city of Marathon to Athens. He ran to deliver the news of the Greek victory over Persia. Before his final stretch, Phillippides had run over 150 miles from Athens to Sparta to request military help. As the legend has it, the Battle of Marathon was the first Greek victory over the Persians, in which Phillippides played a significant role in running long distances to get help and spread the word. This is where the term marathon derives and why it is such an achievement for runners.

By now, maybe you're wondering why this story is relevant to this chapter. The saying, "Life is a marathon, not a sprint," explains that success in life takes intense determination and preparation to go the distance. Three factors are considered, as this saying relates to life; one factor is determination, the other is preparation, and the last is distance. Those who are better prepared and willing to go farther end up getting further ahead than others. Thus, this is the answer to my first question: *with all things equal, what causes one person to go further in life than the other?* The answer, as explained, is in your determination and preparation. Henceforth, your determination (willingness, grit) must come before the preparation to achieve the distance. In other words, your limitations will determine your achievements or lack thereof.

Merriam-Webster defines a limit as *something that bounds, restrains, or confines,* and capability as *the quality or state of being.* Hence, limitless means *without restriction;* limitless capabilities mean *the ability to move without limitations.* Our determination relates to how far we are willing to push ourselves to our limits. This is a straightforward concept, but many people don't fully grasp the power of being limitless. As the Greek messenger, Phillippides acted without limits; you must also be willing to push yourself and train to go the distance. Success is truly a marathon. You have complete control of it, setting the distance of how far you want to go. But you can't try to sprint it, or you will fall short because the preparation is much different. Thus, those who possess the combination of better preparedness and limitlessness will achieve more. They will go further ahead in terms of the marathon because they continue to increase their limits and training. The self-master embraces the marathon, which is how you want to attack life.

Keep Raising the Bar

Have you ever been influenced to stay content with where you are in life? This advice typically sounds something like, "Be happy with what you have.," "Start living in the moment.," or "Stop and smell the roses." While this advice may come with good intentions, it usually does not come from people who have achieved massive success or self-mastery. If so, they may have an ulterior motive or trying to sabotage your journey. These words cannot be farther from the truth. I cannot recall a time in my life when I evolved from being happy with where I was or when I stopped and smelled the roses. In fact, the opposite was true more often than not. The times when I advanced the most happened when I got tired of being content with my current position. I grew and achieved more success each time I pushed myself beyond my current state. Therefore, if you genuinely want to achieve greatness, you must react the same way. You can't let others hinder your progress by feeding you those negative thoughts. Most people don't think that contentment is dangerous to their success, but you are starting to learn better. The fact that you made it to this section puts you into a different category than most, and you are well on your way to improving your life for good.

As you learned in the previous chapter, exemplary

leaders set high expectations for themselves to achieve more. The benefits of doing it greatly outweigh the cons. Depending on how you deal with setbacks, short-term disappointment, patience, or envy of others, you may have some mindfulness exercises to learn. However, these are actually the only adverse outcomes of setting high expectations for yourself. Your success will depend on how much you continue to grow. This growth will not occur when your limits are set too low. You must continue raising the bar repeatedly each time you reach a plateau. Think of it this way—whenever you're stuck, you must break past your barrier to keep going. Some call this "leveling up," Whatever term you want to use, the thought process is the same: You need to raise the bar to advance in all areas. People I have met tend to have mixed feelings about this concept. So, I will share an example so there is no misunderstanding. You can reflect on any similar model that will help you apply it to your life because the concept will remain the same.

If you've ever done physical exercise, specifically strength training, you know how the body reacts to resistance. If you haven't, pay close attention to this example. The individual's goal determines the workout regimen. Thus, if you want to lose weight, overwork your body and change your diet. To get faster, run more often and focus on beating your previous time. In this example, I want to talk about strength. If someone wants to get stronger, they must increase their resistance incrementally. Sometimes, this is done by adding more weight to an exercise, adding more reps or sets, or doing slower reps to add more time. For example, when bench pressing, one strategy weightlifters use is to add more weight to the bar after each set. They will work their way up to their max and then add slightly more weight, say five to ten more pounds. With the help of another person called a "spotter," they will assist the weightlifter with lifting past their maximum resistance level. The weightlifter will use this same strategy for other workouts, and then, after a few weeks, they will become naturally more muscular. By pushing their body past its limit, it will grow, raising its new limit to a higher level. If the weightlifter's former maximum bench press was 300 lbs. without a spotter, but the spotter allowed them to lift 310 lbs. each session, their new max will increase to 310 lbs. Thus, this strategy will improve their strength by increasing their resistance limitation over time.

Keeping consistent improvement at the top of your mind will allow you to improve at whatever you pursue. The mentality is about not giving in to temporary satisfaction. It is about understanding that you must keep adding new goals to your checklist to become more successful. These new goals should always be above the last goal you achieved or complement it, thus forcing you to improve since there will be more resistance. As described in the weightlifting scenario, facing resistance is necessary to advance. This is known as opposition in life, and facing it will make you stronger. So, you must embrace it but do so with a plan to make incremental increases over time. Just like physical fitness goals, your career and lifetime goals can be achieved similarly. You

'Growth will not
occur when your
limits are set
too low.'

can develop a career workout regimen to move ahead. However, living in the moment for too long will stop your growth and many times lead to personal decay because environmental factors will not show you mercy. Keep raising the bar is about your battle with life. The world will continue to evolve, so you must move with more intensity and effort because staying the same person will cause you to fall behind. When you continue raising the bar, you tell life that you are willing to do whatever is necessary to stay ahead. Thus, how far ahead you get will always reflect the effort you put into your growth. Trust me, when you take this approach, you will be delighted with the person you see in the mirror today when comparing them to the person you saw yesterday. At the same time, you will be even more excited to see yourself in the future.

Nothing is Impossible

One of my biggest reasons for pursuing self-mastery occurred years ago when I started noticing the power of endless possibilities. Over the years, I've tested this theory numerous times and continue to reach the same conclusion that nothing is impossible. In my day-to-day work, I manage and oversee operations, which includes finding solutions and better efficiencies to run businesses. I've done this work for over a decade in many industries and continue improving with time. My expertise involves overcoming challenges, and I am literally in the business of breaking impossibilities. As I grew in my roles, I began applying the same efforts I used in business to my lifestyle and discovered a drastic change. I realized that all of life's challenges were conquerable. I found that virtually nothing was impossible. Think about it. What challenges do you currently face in your industry and life in general? Wouldn't you agree that these challenges are simply problems that require a solution? So, then the answer becomes finding the best solution. Most solutions derive from gathering your needed resources and developing an action plan. Resources don't have to be tangible items like money, supplies, and equipment; they can be intangible, like knowledge, motivation, skills, partnerships, etc. Therefore, impossibilities realistically don't exist; they only exist to the limit you are willing to overcome them. In other words, if your limits are greater than your obstacles, you can surmount them.

As I mentioned, I've tested this theory endlessly. I've also watched my top-tiered colleagues and others put it to the test. Top performers in any industry also provide evidence that supports this concept, but people don't want to accept it for what it is because it's really a straightforward approach. Believing that nothing is impossible explains how athletes break records, how new inventions are created, and how industry leaders continue dominating their competition. The truth is, when you expand your limitations, you will get past what's in your way with the right resources and a solid plan. The focus then becomes gathering the resources you need because you already accepted that it is possible to get past what you face. This focal shift is a key to unlimited success and will save you time if you learn it now. Please pay close attention to what I will explain next because I don't want you to miss this invaluable advice.

In the words of Nelson Mandela, *"It always seems impossible until it's done."* This statement is true on many levels, and you just read that impossibilities are surmountable when your limitations are set above your barriers. However, that explains how to overcome what's in front of you. What if nothing was in your way and you had no problems to solve or barriers to overcome? That's usually not the case, but at times it can be. This rhetorical question will help you wrap your head around the following statement. The same way you expand your limits to overcome impossibilities is the same way you can create possibilities. Possibilities are best described as opportunities or positive alternatives. They are not given; they are manufactured intentionally or unintentionally. The wise and successful spend time ensuring their possibilities are under their control. They do so by engaging in the following:

1. Identifying a goal
2. Setting their mental and physical limitations past the goal
3. Aligning and gathering their resources
4. Developing an action plan

The last thing you want to do is leave things up to chance. Why do that when you have every right to control your destiny? When you can get out of your own way, you will realize how happier you are and how life keeps working in your favor. You will surely start living toward your purpose when you begin believing you can overcome the impossible and create what is possible. Until then, you are limiting your potential.

Why People Set Personal Limitations

You're going to start seeing a trend as I explain the first common reason why people set personal limitations. You shouldn't be surprised by this, but I still think it's essential to call it out. A common reason people set personal limits is that—you guessed it, THEY'RE LAZY! As you recall from the situational awareness chapter, many individuals avoid doing things that require extra work. This is the same case for setting personal limitations. Taking the easy road is far less demanding than putting in the time and energy to raise your limits. However, what you put into your success is what you will get from it. Therefore, those who do the bare minimum and just enough to get by are far less successful than those who go the extra mile, especially when faced with hardship. Look around you, and I'm sure you'll see signs of this everywhere. I have had people tell me they set low expectations to trick themselves into believing they overachieved something. In reality, this strategy sets them back and only produces short-term gratification. Individuals who do this don't even realize they are running a continuous loop because there is no growth in developing low expectations. This mindset is, *"I'll just take what I can get"* instead of *"I'm going to push myself as hard as I can."* Which thought process do you think produces better results when the end product is the level of success?

Another reason people set personal limitations is because they struggle to seek additional resources. Earlier in this chapter, I explained how critical it is to find the right resources. The lack of them disrupts solutions and becomes a massive barrier. Coincidently, it becomes a roadblock to other obstacles many people already face. Nonetheless, this issue forces many to set limits because they just can't get the help they need. Some may be afraid to ask for it, and others may be too prideful to. They may also not know where to look for additional resources to help solve their problems or create opportunities. This is also a significant concern when developing any plan because a plan is only as solid as its foundation. An excellent example of limits set to avoid seeking additional resources is when business owners don't expand because they can't grow their teams. So, instead, they find comfort where they are and make statements like, *"I'm making good money anyway."* In reality, they're settling because they have reached their limit. Instead, if they raised their limits, they would do whatever it takes to fill the gap. For example, they would study better recruitment strategies or attend networking events to connect with like-minded people and build partnerships. The point is that many people don't do these things because something prevents them. You can avoid this concern as you continue your path of self-mastery and learn how to conquer fearlessness. Fearlessness will help you raise your limits and prevent this common barrier altogether. You will learn more about it in the following chapter.

There are many personal reasons individuals set limitations. But the last explanation I want you to be aware of is that they are scared of failure. Society will make you think you've failed when you don't accomplish something. However, the only time you actually fail is when you quit. Failures and quitters are the same because they both reach their limits and then discontinue their objectives. On the other hand, it is not a failure if you fall and keep going; it's only a setback. Hence, since setbacks are stressful and complicated, people avoid them and feel better by lowering their expectations. They're not willing to risk falling short of their goals, so they reduce their limits, causing them to reduce their goals. If you can relate to this reason or know someone who can ask them or yourself the following question— Who achieves more, the person who reached for a ten but landed at eight, or the person who went for a seven and made it? This question is a simple method I use to exercise my willingness. Sometimes, it's a quick reality check like this that we all can use to help charge our drive.

How to Raise Your Limitations

Hopefully, you've had some "ah ha" moments as you progressed through this chapter. I'll be the first to admit that embracing this way of life is not easy, but it is possible. (You see how I snuck that in there?) With all seriousness, developing limitless capabilities requires much work because it goes against our natural tendencies. Naturally, the human body is built to protect the owner. One of the functions of the brain is to detect threats, which then triggers the fight, flight or freeze hormone. As I explained, when setbacks occur, they can be highly stressful situations. Therefore, the automatic stress response becomes flight, and individuals take the first opportunity to avoid those scenarios. However, we can train our brains to react differently. Raising your limitations requires training your brain to remain in the fight state to overcome setbacks instead of running from them. The following tips will help you develop this skill.

1. **Identify the worst outcomes**

   a. One of the most vital lessons I learned in my military training is the benefits of thinking about the worst outcomes. When faced with a challenge, tough decision, or any form of opposition, identifying the worst consequences of the scenario will put things into proper perspective. You force your brain into "fight mode" by looking at the worst outcomes. Exercising this ability will better prepare you to move forward by alerting your senses to possible threats.

b. This reverse psychology method will train you to find solutions instead of excuses. It will help you to develop a pros versus cons list of anything you intend to pursue. I recommend writing this down for all the tough decisions you face, whether starting a new career or business or deciding on new software in a corporate setting. Doing this will help you evaluate whether the path is worth it and show you where your current limit lies. When you physically see the pros and cons, it will allow you to raise your limits or shift plans in your assessment.

2. Change your inner circle

a. One of the quickest changes and most impactful things you can do to raise your limits is to change your inner circle. Sure, many believe their lifelong friends positively influence their lives, but if they are not pushing them to grow, it is time to move on. You cannot let anyone pull you down or hold you back if you want to reach your maximum potential. Changing your inner circle to develop relationships with like-minded people is a guaranteed way to expand your limits. It will show you that what you believe is complicated may be simple for others.

b. Social media has made networking more accessible than ever, and I recommend searching for events in your industry to connect with others. Be sure to avoid blogs and hostile groups because these are also easy to get into. Do your research and ensure the events you attend are structured, well-intentioned, and educational. The last thing you want to do is join a group of complainers that will lower your limits.

3. Celebrate your small wins

a. I know the feeling of pursuing a massive goal can be demanding. Often, it seems like no light is at the end of the tunnel. Being so focused on the long-term goals can adversely impact you if you do not take the time to enjoy the small wins. As I pursued my education and business ventures, I learned to celebrate my small victories. Passing a course with an A, reaching a new business milestone, or completing a project all call for celebration, even though you may still need to meet the main objective.

b. Find out what motivates you and will allow you to develop a celebratory process. It can be having a toast with your significant other, having a dinner party with your family or team, buying yourself something new, or anything that makes you happy. The point is that you must make this intentional and prepare to do something to congratulate yourself. You are working hard and deserve to do this for yourself. Doing so will keep you motivated.

4. **Keep track of your progress**

   a. *"You can't really know where you are going until you know where you have been."*—Maya Angelo

   This critical step will keep you aware of progress. As you continue to grow, tough times will make you second-guess your journey. Keeping track of your progress will keep you on pace and motivate you. You see how much you achieved each time you reflect on your origins. Some will claim this is boastful, but doing it will continue feeding your growth.

   b. There are many ways to keep track of your progress in today's age. You can use online tools to create timelines and document your journey. There are also more subtle ways, like hanging up certificates, framing letters, and creating anniversary celebrations. These are all ways that act as quick reminders to inform you of your progress, and trust me, they work! The excitement you will get from doing this will empower you to strive for more because you will remember what you went through and know you are capable of much more.

5. **Build your confidence**

a. You will struggle to raise your limits if you lack confidence. People who do not believe in themselves certainly do not push themselves to their limits because they fear embarrassment and failure. Lack of confidence derives from inexperience and lack of knowledge. Thus, you can only raise your limits if prepared to face what lies beyond them. As I explained in the How to Become an Exemplary Leader section, you must continue educating yourself to build your confidence.

b. The more you overcome, the more your confidence will grow. Don't expect to know everything, but gain general knowledge about your path and build on it. Suppose you face what some consider impossible or are trying to create an opportunity. In that case, you must indulge yourself in learning about it, or you will give up easily. Don't set yourself up for failure by ignoring the requirements of achieving your goal. Often, all it takes is gaining a little more knowledge than you had yesterday to feel more confident today.

When the world is filled with many people who will only take so much, those who go the extra mile gain everything. The distractions of this generation do not have to hinder your progress, and you have learned that success comes in many forms. Impossibilities only exist if you let them, and possibilities are attainable if you reach for them. The quality of your life depends on the personal limits you set for yourself; the higher they are, the more you will advance. Unfortunately, the same can be said for setting low limits; low limits produce a lower quality of life. If you want to break the cycle and achieve unlimited success, you must put all your efforts into acquiring the skill of limitless capabilities. So, practice raising your limits, and you will see drastic improvements in your life. The skills learned in this chapter work collaboratively with what you will learn in the following chapter about fearlessness.

4

Living Without Fear

Atychiphobia– The Fear of Failure

What comes to mind when you think of your biggest fears? If failure falls at the top of your list, you are not alone. In fact, a recent survey of over one thousand people concluded that 31% of adults face a fear of failure. How does that reality compare to those you know and interact with? This fear has become so common that psychologists and psychiatrists have begun studying it deeper to understand the triggers and complexity of this phenomenon. The fear of failure can have many levels, from mild to highly severe. Those who experience severe cases of fear of failure are said to suffer from Atychiphobia because it is long-term and has a negative life impact. Atychiphobia is a condition where someone fears failure so intensely that it causes them to become non-productive. Individuals with this condition are known to be extreme procrastinators, avoiders, delegators, and pessimists. As you learned about limitless capabilities in the previous chapter, you discovered that people who fear failure also set low expectations for themselves. Ironically, those who suffer from Atychiphobia become failures due to their non-responsiveness to handling tasks and seeking opportunities. They end up paralyzing themselves socially and professionally and, without help, eventually, fall into the same trap they tried avoiding.

There are many contributors to Atychiphobia. Some who face it may have experienced too many failed attempts at passionate goals or witnessed their loved ones and colleagues fail numerous times. They also may believe they are incapable of being successful or are too focused on being a perfectionist. As discussed previously, it's natural to fear a challenge or stressful situation. However, worrying about it to the point of incapacity is dangerous and deadly to your career. Another significant contributor to Atychiphobia in today's society is social media. I've spoken much about positive and adverse uses of social media, but some people are fans of others so intensely that they never believe they can come close to their success levels. Therefore, they develop their fear of failure by unrealistically comparing themselves, not considering the journey their social media influencer went through or the resources they may have. This thinking causes them to forgo all motivation because they have already decided that what they will amount to will never be close to those they may follow. If you know anyone like this, a good reality check and wake-up call could be just the push they need.

People with Atychiphobia have described their symptoms as tightness in their chest, high anxiety, panic, trembling, dizziness, depression, and paranoia, to name a few. Many cases also lead to drug abuse, anger, and social withdrawal. I point out all these problems to alert you to the truth of the fear of failure so you can monitor yourself and your loved ones more closely. Failure is scary, and the average person does not know how to handle or avoid it. But you are not average and can avoid ending up in this category. Your journey of self-mastery is preparing you to build the attributes of fearlessness. The more you study these ten pillars, the more you bypass the traps that mediocre thinkers fall into. Atychiphobia is a mental prison that destroys success. Understanding the true meaning of fear will help you connect more closely with becoming fearless. Hence, Merriam-Webster defines fear as *"an unpleasant often strong emotion caused by anticipation or awareness of danger."* Fearless is described as being brave and free from fear. Thus, achieving self-mastery will allow you to develop fearlessness, which I define as *the art of overcoming and facing fear head-on.* Now, let's dive deeper into how you can live a successful life without fear.

Fight, Flight, or Freeze

One of the most critical steps I offered you to learn how to raise your limits was identifying the worst outcomes to force your brain into "fight mode." This triggering approach not only works for raising your limits, but the hormone responsible for it can also help you face your fears. For my healthcare gurus out there, this section is not meant to become a medical journal but a way to learn about the power of activating this acute stress response to become fearless—people who live fearlessly learn how to command this response at will by training their automatic nervous system. They know how to use it for offense, while most only use it defensively. Some of the most successful people have mastered this technique, many without realizing it, but I'm here to explain how.

Think about a time when you faced an unfamiliar, life-changing event in your professional life. You may have had an important interview, the first day of a new job, a performance, a presentation to give, or a critical business meeting. Whatever comes to mind, I want you to think about your emotions leading up to the day. What were your thoughts up until the very moment you faced it? What was the outcome? Most people will agree that they were stressed out and even dreaded the decision to continue. They will say that their heart was racing, they were sick to their stomach, or other descriptions of anxiety. They may also agree that the outcome was average, could have been better, or that they tried their best. However, very few people would say they were excited, eager, and had no worries at all. This minority group would express that they "knocked it out of the park," exceeded expectations, or even impressed themselves. They would show no signs of stress. Instead, they would show signs of joy and a hunger for more. This latter group describes the fearless and how the same scenario can produce drastically different results.

Considering the previous example, this captures the difference in the reaction to what is known as the fight, flight, or freeze hormone. I've personally benefited from gaining control over this reaction, which has made me fearless in many ways. The most significant benefit is that I have created new opportunities by being willing to make sacrifices and outperforming others who approach the same scenarios with fear. In other words, controlling the stress hormone will help you transcend your peers and allow you to take advantage of opportunities. Others will empower you, and doors will open because they know you won't be afraid of what you may see when you walk through them. You will develop fearlessness to the point where it will help you turn your stressful situations into everyday situations to react better. Imagine how much better your life would be if your automatic response became an offensive position instead of a defensive one when stressful events occurred. Your achievements would be

'High achievers do everything possible to create the scenarios they will face beforehand.'

endless because you would face your fears head-on without worry. Your mind, body, and spirit would be aligned, allowing you to perform at your peak level.

How people control the fight, flight or freeze response is commonly witnessed in combat sports. Let's discuss boxing, for example. There are some exceptions for the naturally gifted, but most of the world's best boxers know how to tap into their fight hormone at will. They become champions as a result of the work they put in outside the ring. Champion boxers study countless hours of their opponents' recent fights to learn their moves and discover their weaknesses. They study their opponents' style so intensely that they know how many seconds it takes them to throw a fully extended punch and how often they throw their jab versus their power punches. When training, champion boxers even spar against fighters who closely match their upcoming opponent—They try to match stature, style, power, speed, and abilities. When the day of the fight comes, they are well prepared because they've considered all scenarios they may face against their opponent. Thus, they enter the fight composed and at their peak level because they know what they may expect. The boxer is then able to trigger their hormonal response to release adrenaline to heighten their senses, putting them in what some would describe as a "god-like" state.

While you may not consider taking up boxing or any combat sport, the thought process and concept are the same that apply to reaching your goals. The highest achievers and successful people trigger their hormonal response the same, allowing them to handle highly stressful situations with ease. When they are aware of a new challenge or opportunity, they spend rigorous hours preparing for it. For example, when preparing for a business meeting, they think about all the challenging questions that may come up and develop multiple answers for them. They consider rebuttals and ensure they address everything relevant to the discussion. They may do mock business meetings, talk to themselves in the mirror, search the internet for related information, basically anything they can do to create a similar scenario. When the time comes for their meeting, they walk in confident and well-prepared to face the challenge. The preparation starts this fearlessness. High achievers do everything possible to create the scenarios they will face beforehand. They can literally see themselves in the future moment because they know what it will look like. Some even know the exact outfit they will wear and where they will sit or stand in the room. I've personally taken these steps throughout my career and find them most helpful. This intense preparation has been the most significant contributor to my fearlessness. Controlling the acute stress response will make you unstoppable, and you will achieve your goals more frequently by being better prepared.

Competition is the Best Medicine

Nowadays, it's become acceptable to be a loser. The world has gone soft; society has made it okay to ignore and downplay winning. Well, I'm here to tell you that winning should be the only acceptable outcome in your mind! If you're one of those people who believe in participation trophies and awards for all competitors, then you will struggle to achieve self-mastery. The self-master pushes themself to be great at every opportunity they have. They embody being a winner and look at losing as a way to improve and do better next time. Successful people do not always win; in fact, they lose often. However, they learn from losing and continue to perform better because they love the taste of victory. When people receive awards for losing, it deceives their minds into working less hard. Thus, it creates a society of mediocre people who don't compete and don't care about winning. On the other hand, competition is healthy and forces individuals to higher levels because the winner always wants the reward. Therefore, competition is the best medicine for someone who lacks fearlessness. If you're the type that backs down to opposition because you don't want to become arrogant or don't want people to view you as a show-off or whatever reason you designed in your mind, then you need to think differently. You must accept that people will judge you either way. So, why not be deemed as an overachiever or a show-off? The truth is, you will achieve more, and only those who are guilty of underachieving or competing against you will be negative about it. Do you honestly think your stakeholders will be upset with you for blowing your competition out of the water? Of course not.

It's a proven fact that developing a competitive nature produces positive results. Life is a continuous competition, and you should embrace it. The winners live prosperous lives of freedom and reward. They earn more and can do more for their families because they do not accept losing. I want to be clear that you shouldn't break the law and cheat others to compete; however, you should exploit every resource and misstep of your competitors. This is what big businesses do and how they capture market share. Industry leaders exploit the weaknesses of their competitors. The competition drives innovation because each company fights to gain industry control. As the tug of war continues, the companies push one another higher, producing better products and services for all customers. This competitive relationship should be the same for humanity. As you compete with others, your beneficiaries will benefit. Your fears will dissipate because your competitive nature will take over, and you will see life's challenges as winnable situations. Here's a reality check to remember: Whether you compete or not, others will still compete against you. In this world, you can choose to become a predator, prey, or bystander. That is the true American dream because many countries don't have the luxury of choice. The citizens are sometimes born into wealth or poverty and can't control this choice. So, either you choose to compete, or others will choose for you, and you will become a bystander of their success.

The last takeaway of competition I want you to understand is how beneficial it is to your self-development. The previous paragraphs described the positive impacts of competition on society. However, as you feed your competitive nature, you will start to compete with yourself. You will not only compete with others but also want to try outdoing yourself. This is the ultimate competitive level you wish to ascend to. The hunger for competition will be so ingrained in your life that you will develop habits that will force you to try and one-up yourself. High achievers understand this power and consistently apply it to goal-setting. They feed their competitive beast so often that it looks for ways to allow them to keep climbing higher and higher. Therefore, because so many people choose to become bystanders and not compete, the high achiever discovers they can get endless enjoyment from internal competition. Understanding this concept explains why the wealth gap continues to expand. It happens because those at the top continue competing with one another, but ultimately themselves. With all said, you owe it to yourself and your family to develop a competitive nature. It is a crucial ingredient of fearlessness.

Why People Struggle to Become Fearless

Have you thought about your purpose today? One of the main reasons people don't become fearless is that their "why" isn't strong enough. Suppose you don't think about your "why" each day; you will temporarily lose sight of your objective. Individuals who live without fear are passionate about their purpose and dedicate their lives to it. They don't let fear get in the way of their goals because they pursue them as if their life depends on it. And in many ways, it does! When you serve a purpose greater than you, you don't worry about what barriers exist. You are ready to take on the world, and you don't let your emotions or anything disrupt your path. Conversely, people who live in fear let excuses overtake them. They haven't identified a just cause for which they are willing to do anything. Therefore, it becomes easy to let any obstacle get in their way. They will never become fearless because they turn the other way when facing opposition. They are more likely to give up on difficult goals and always choose the path of least resistance.

There's also a lack of fearless people in this world because many don't want to make sacrifices. Facing challenges head-on requires multiple sacrifices. You must sacrifice time, comfort, objects, and often relationships. Making advancements frequently entails stepping out of their comfort zone; those without fearlessness simply don't want to do it. They are not blind to what it takes to move forward but have accepted staying in their lane, even though it means they will keep their same income and problems. There are enough success stories out there to know that, most times, you have to change to become great. However, people who live in fear are more comfortable staying who they are and avoid getting rid of bad habits or giving up things to improve. I've witnessed people sabotage their careers because they didn't want more responsibilities or to put more thought into their work. Instead, they remained in the same position for years while making the same complaints. It becomes a vicious cycle and an addiction. The fearless, however, develop an attitude of doing whatever it takes to win, knowing they must make sacrifices. They are ready to give up who they are for what they will become. They are addicted to the journey and understand that sacrifices are necessary to obtain their desired life.

How many people do you know that believe their fate is already written? Hopefully, you're not one who thinks this way. This way of thinking is adversarial to fearlessness. I'm here to debunk the myth that humankind has no control over its destiny. What you do today determines where you end up tomorrow. You have a choice to become great and change your future. If controlling your destiny works for negative things, why wouldn't it for positive outcomes? Think about this: if you broke the law today, you would be punished and likely end up in jail tomorrow. This is a simple cause-

and-effect relationship. It works the same for positive outcomes like goal setting and achievement. So, when people claim their fate is already written, it makes no sense, and you should challenge this notion. When others believe their story is already written, they will not pursue anything with total effort. They will never gain fearlessness because they think they can live and end up where they are supposed to be, as if life works that way. Sometimes, they may put effort into something and try achieving goals, but whenever they are challenged, the negative thought will take over, and they will back down. Many believe that life happens and let it pass them by. You should never think this way because it is a virus that will cause you to waste your limited time on this earth. If you want to become fearless, think the opposite and take control!

How to Live Without Fear

Fearlessness is viewed as one of the most valuable characteristics one can have. It is also known as bravery, courageousness, lionheartedness, boldness, and having guts. Throughout this chapter, you learned numerous reasons why becoming fearless is essential to your career. There is no simple recipe for it because being courageous is a habit, and with patterns, one must make intentional efforts over time. But you can evolve into a fearless being with hard work and persistence. I shared a few reasons I've witnessed why people don't become fearless, but there are so many others. Being fearless should not be confused with recklessness. Some try to connect the two, but there is a clear difference. Fearlessness entails taking calculated risks without hesitation, while recklessness is taking uncalculated risks. Recklessness is walking directly into danger with no plan and requires no skill. The fearless move with finesse and calculation because they are prepared, experienced, and typically make good decisions. Here are a few ways that you can begin developing this characteristic.

1. **Maintain good health**

    a. Taking challenges head-on is a daunting task and requires much energy. Often, being fearless is mentally and physically draining because you work against resistance. Thus, maintaining good health is optimal and will help you keep going. You should eat healthy, develop a consistent exercise routine, and stick to it. Maintaining good health will keep you sharp and allow you to perform tasks at your peak abilities.

b. If you do not care for your health, you will struggle to help others. You can't achieve your goals if you're in the hospital and don't have the energy to work toward them. Maintaining good health is your best defense for fighting aging and common illnesses. Going through your exercise routine will also give you the time to separate from your work. It will give you a well-needed break to refresh and refocus on objectives.

2. **Visualize yourself in the moment**

a. This step is critical to developing fearlessness. If you can't visualize yourself in the moment, you won't physically get there. This practice is the main contributor to my personal success, and I would bet my life on it that it works. Whatever the objective, whether evaluating a new career, business idea, promotion, etc., you must see yourself there first.

b. Spend as much time as possible running through alternatives in your mind. Sometimes, you have time to decide, but often, your time is limited, so mastering this technique will help you make quick decisions when necessary. You will learn how to quickly analyze multiple choices to envision possible outcomes of each decision. This helps build fearlessness because you will gain confidence and trust in your decision-making.

3. **Discover small opportunities to step up**

   a. As you've learned, being fearless is a habit. To develop this habit, you need countless opportunities to practice. Hence, it is essential to identify small opportunities that require bravery. Stepping up at work to lead a new project, volunteering to lead a group, becoming a mentor, and teaching your loved ones to be brave are all examples of things you can do to build your fearlessness.

   b. The more you take on leadership challenges, as mentioned, the more you will grow your fearless nature. Volunteering for these small opportunities to lead will evolve into massive ones. This practice will become a way of life and is one of the most effective ways to create courageous habits. The approach utilizes a compounding effect by taking your small, fearless ventures and multiplying them, producing a bold individual ready to take on the world.

4. **Reconnect with your pain**

   a. When those moments test you, and you feel like giving up, you must reconnect with your pain and recall what going backward felt like. The feeling of pain, frustration, and going through the thoughts of your past situations can be traumatic, but it can also be used as motivation. When tough times require courage, you can look forward to pressing on because the pain of dealing with your past is much worse.

   b. Reconnecting with your pain forces you to move ahead because you never want to feel the stress and tough times again. Practicing this approach is helpful, but be sure to dwell in the past for only a short time without taking action. The point of this exercise is to use your history to fuel your future. When done right, you will remind yourself that accomplishing what's ahead of you may be challenging, but your past life, fighting bad habits, struggling to pay bills, and financial distress feel more painful. These thoughts will give you the boost you need to make your next move.

5. **Worry about what's in your control**

   a. People fear the unknown, which prevents them from trying new things. Many things in life are beyond your control, but there are also so many that you can affect. Spend your time focusing all your efforts on what's in your control, and you will realize that you can change your reality. You can control your thoughts, energy, knowledge, and action. Therefore, the efforts you put into your next move will impact the outcome.

b. By understanding and accepting that no one knows what tomorrow holds, you should put your best foot forward today. Too many think about making mistakes and worry themselves to death. You should only be worried about your contributions to your future and let the rest take care of itself. Those who live fearlessly and achieve self-mastery are well aware of this correlation. They let their actions guide them to endless accomplishments and promising futures.

You must be willing to do whatever it takes to achieve your goals. You should get used to taking risks and betting on yourself if you want to live out your dreams. When you are afraid to advance and hesitate too long, you will see others take advantage of your missteps. Don't let people steal your opportunities because you fear failure, sacrifice, or the unknown. The courageous will always prevail, and fearlessness is a rare characteristic. However, you are capable of acquiring it by following the steps mentioned and studying this chapter until it becomes habitual. Living without fear will take you to places you never thought possible and allow you to obtain things others will never receive because the path is uncommon. The course of self-mastery requires it, and the rewards are captivating. Becoming fearless will benefit those you interact with; many will put their faith and trust in you to lead and handle tasks. You will become the star player worth betting on in the professional world, and in your personal life, nothing will stand in your way.

5

Mindset is Everything

The Placebo Effect

"Before a brain can register a thought, a mind must think it... every step of the way is mind over matter... We override our brains all the time."
—Deepak Chopra, MD.

The mind is the ultimate control system, and perception is reality. Before new medications enter the market, they must undergo human clinical trials to determine their effectiveness and impact on the subjects. Many know that if the experimental drug has deadly side effects or does not work for its intended use, it will not pass the trials; thus, it will not enter the market and will be discarded. However, understanding how the drugs go through testing during clinical trials is not commonly known. Pay close attention to the following explanation, as it will help you understand the power of the mind:

During clinical trials, researchers, including doctors, technicians, and administrators, gather a group of volunteers to undergo treatment by conducting double-blinded studies. The studies are called double-blinded because the researchers split the volunteers into two randomized groups, with both unaware of which one they belong to. One group receives the experimental drug, while the other gets a "placebo." A placebo is a replication of the drug being tested without any of the pharmaceutical ingredients. Many refer to a placebo as a "sugar pill" because it mainly comprises the pill's casing and inactive ingredients like sugar and other substances. Hence, to test the experimental drug's effectiveness, its results are recorded and compared to those of the placebo. As mentioned, both volunteer groups are unaware whether they received the placebo or the experimental drug. Therefore, after testing, the medication is said to be effective if the participants' reaction to it is greater than the reaction of the placebo group. These placebo tests occur during Phase I of a III-Phase clinical trial testing required for FDA approval. Notably, only 33% of experimental drugs that pass Phase I will pass Phase II of the placebo trials.

The placebo effect is the human reaction to a placebo, and this concept has been around for centuries. Using placebos in clinical trials has been the gold standard since post-World War II. Placebos are still used in numerous clinical trials, including cancer treatment, pain treatment, and Parkinson's, to name a few. You may wonder how and why a fake pill is commonly used to test vital experimental drugs and why the success rates are highly impacted. This answer is due to the participants' perceptions and expectations. The volunteers genuinely believe they receive the experimental drug during these placebo clinical trials because of what they are told. Before giving the placebo, the doctors explain the treatment benefits of the experimental drug and potential outcomes, such as reduced pain. Hearing the health benefits and treatment results beforehand, the volunteers expect the pill to work, regardless of whether they received the placebo or experimental drug. In most cases, the treatment results are positive for both participant groups if the doctor provides positive information, has reasonable bedside manner, and the clinical environment is comforting. Nonetheless, if the experimental drug outperforms the placebo, it moves to Phase III.

The phenomenon of the placebo effect is so impactful because it proves that the mind produces positive or negative physical responses based on the information it receives. This response works both ways, and researchers also conduct studies to test for negative results. For example, in 2017, a research team conducted a small placebo test using an antihistamine placebo cream to treat an allergic reaction caused by a skin injection in the arm. The doctor told their participants that the cream would help their rash while telling others it would worsen it. After testing, the research team discovered that the group they gave the positive information to experienced a reduction in the size of their rashes; thus, a positive reaction. In contrast, the group who received the negative drug description from the doctor experienced an increase in the size of their rashes, thereby, an adverse response. In this experiment, both groups received only a placebo cream. The team then proceeded further in this study. When including other factors like a concerned, competent doctor in one group versus the same doctor acting inexperienced, even wearing a nametag displaying "student doctor," the results correlated even more to positive and negative outcomes. There are thousands of similar studies out there that prove this phenomenon.

The ultimate improvement ability was not based on experimental drugs or placebos in the previous examples. These experiments display the true power of mindset. According to Merriam-Webster, mindset is *"a fixed state of mind."* I believe mindset goes beyond that and is best described as *the reality of one's thoughts and beliefs.* As you think about the placebo effect and how it is used to push experimental drugs forward or discredit them, the same trials can be conducted in your personal and professional life. Harnessing the placebo effect can help individuals achieve goals by believing in their abilities and being optimistic about their attempts. However, it does not end with the way of thinking. The environment and those involved in the objective also contribute to the outcome. Therefore, to produce the best results, you must genuinely believe in the entire process of your pursuit. You must think positively about your team, partners, and your plan. You must entertain positive thoughts, conversations, and the information entering your mind when attacking your goals. The placebo effect has been tried and tested and is accurate. It is also a double-edged sword, so protecting your mind from negativity and disbelief is best because it can hinder you. However, when exercised correctly, you can overcome your struggles and produce better outcomes by applying the placebo effect to your lifestyle. Just remember that this only works when you remain genuinely optimistic, and by combining the other pillars of self-mastery, you can do so with ease.

The Universal Law of Attraction

Understanding the placebo effect will prepare you for this section and help you conceptualize the universal law of attraction. As you learned early on in this book, all situations are unique, so trying to do exactly what works for some may play out differently in your case. This is why achieving self-mastery is a formula: one pillar supports the other, and so on. Therefore, you must constantly analyze your situation to know your next move. By always being aware of your contributions, thoughts, actions, and input, you can devise the best course for you to reach success. Many have heard about the universal law of attraction in some form or fashion. Maybe you believe in it, and perhaps you don't. However, I am here to help you discern the truth and how this philosophy can benefit your life.

The universal law of attraction comes from one of the twelve universal laws accepted throughout history. The law of attraction originated in the late 1800s. Its concepts have been linked to Hermeticism and are deeply tied to Sir Issac Newtown's law of gravity, explaining that all objects attract in proportion to the product of their masses. Similarly, the law of attraction suggests that humans attract what they put into the universe, both positive and negative. This philosophy has multiple layers: ***magnetism, manifestation,*** *alignment,* and *karma*. In other words, the law of attraction explains that the universe engages in fair exchange with humankind. The root of the law of attraction is the mind, and it is the driving force that ignites the universal response. Thus, having the right mindset dictates positive outcomes and vice versa. While the law of attraction is controversial, one of the most common myths is that individuals only have to think positively, and the rest will take care of itself. The law of attraction does not work that way, so let's explore some examples of how it actually works.

Magnetism: Magnetism describes the connection between attracting like things. One of the clearest examples of this power occurs when you purchase or are looking for a new car. Recall the last time you bought a new car or started shopping for one. Shortly afterward, sometimes even on the drive home or as soon as you hit the road, you repeatedly see the same car. Coincidently, you see the same model more than you've ever seen it before. I'm sure I can't be the only one this happens to; in fact, I know I'm not. The explanation for this occurrence is because of magnetism. In this example, you attract the same car because you continue thinking about it. Your thoughts produce a response from the universe to allow you to attract what you're mainly thinking about. Through magnetism, you actually begin seeking what you're thinking about. In this case, you unconsciously start looking for the car, allowing you to see it more frequently. When you apply magnetism to your career, it helps you to seek out the opportunities

'Alignment, as it refers to the law of attraction, means to be in sync with your thoughts and surroundings to draw energy from them.'

you think mainly about. It allows you to spot the things you think primarily about when you would otherwise overlook them or question them. In contrast to positive thinking, negative thoughts about opportunities allow you only to see the bad because you attract it. People who think negatively often struggle to see positive signs even when they're directly in front of them.

Manifestation: Manifestation goes more profound than the thought process described in magnetism. It is the belief and total acceptance of one's thoughts. This layer takes thinking to the next level, where thoughts take shape and become words and actions. Manifestation requires one to start verbalizing one's thoughts and manifesting them. It allows individuals to say what they want and not just think about it. You may have heard people refer to this as "putting it into the universe." You want to get to the point where magnetism and manifestation work congruently. Positive manifesting is intentional and requires reinforcing phrases like "I will," "I can," and "I am." Be careful not to use terms like "I won't," "I can't," and "I'm not" when referring to your career or aspirations. Many other favorable terms can be used to manifest, but these are some that can get you going down the right path. Ensure you do not follow positive phrases with negative adverbs like "I will never" or the universe will pay it back to you. Manifesting positive outcomes also incorporates conversing and writing; exercising both methods can be more advantageous. After you've attracted an opportunity, you will want to whole-heartedly talk about it wholeheartedly and discuss how and why you will succeed.

Alignment: Aligning one's thoughts with one's surroundings is where I often see shortcomings. I frequently see gaps in their alignment in talking with my clients and mentees about their goals. The law of attraction will not work without alignment because magnetism and manifestation will not work in the wrong environment. Alignment, as it refers to the law of attraction, means to be in sync with your thoughts and surroundings to draw energy from them. It means putting yourself in the most optimal position to attract and manifest in the environment best suited for your goals. A straightforward way to understand alignment is to consider the previous examples about the new car or career opportunities. If you live in a densely populated low-income community or the middle of the desert, you will less frequently see the new vehicle you're thinking about. Or if you're an ambitious person practicing magnetism and manifestation to land your dream job but work for an organization that is not growing and rarely hires the position you're looking for, then you are in misalignment. Therefore, you will not attract the opportunities you want if the environment cannot support them. I realize that, in theory, this is simple; however, it may be challenging in practice. Many people can't just get up and go to the best environment to support their goals, but they can progress by being active, making connections with others on the same path, and keeping a positive mindset.

Karma: In the universal law of attraction, karma describes the continuous relationship between cause and effect. Karma is not magic; instead, it's the energy you put out that comes back to you. Many views about karma exist, but I've learned through experience that it works harmoniously with magnetism and manifestation. In the previous chapter, *Living Without Fear*, I briefly explained how karma relates to fearlessness and discredits the myth that our futures are set in stone. This is accurate because the world functions through energy. Our thoughts, feelings, and actions are all sources of energy that we extrapolate into the universe. As we release energy, we create room for other energy sources to replace what was lost. The human body is designed always to attempt to replace what it loses and look for energy sources to fill the void. It tries to replace it with matching energy, whether positive or negative. Therefore, the things you do today, your thoughts, and how you treat people will affect you in the future. I practice getting good karma because I know this all to be true. By understanding the fundamentals of karma, you can begin small experiments to test it out and then expand as you evolve. You will discover that it's not magic but science and psychology.

Fixed, Growth, and Victim Mindsets

By now, you should know that the mind is the root of all our problems and successes. The mindset is everything, and as you become a self-master, you must gain mindfulness to reach your maximum level. The concepts of the Mindful pillar of self-mastery go back to early history as you have learned and are widely studied. So, what is mindfulness, and how does it relate to mindset? Merriam-Webster defines mindfulness as *"the practice of maintaining a nonjudgmental state of heightened or complete awareness of one's thoughts, emotions, or experiences on a moment-to-moment basis."* I agree with this definition and further emphasize *"complete awareness."* Being mindful allows one to control one's mindset and use it to improve their life. Now that you know mindfulness, let's explore the three different mindsets one can have.

The most common mindsets are fixed and growth. Throughout my career, I have learned another that deserves attention and exists among individuals: the victim mindset. Each person you interact with will exhibit one of these three mindsets. As I explain them, try to discover which one you identify with to know how to deal with it. First, the fixed mindset describes people who believe that individuals are born with all the life skills they will need. They think one's creator embedded precisely what they need in their DNA and thus do not believe people can change. The fixed minders are more likely to give up on unfamiliar things and only stay in their comfort zone. This group is incapable of aligning with fearlessness, exemplary leadership, or any other pillars of self-mastery. Fixed-minded people can become successful. However, they will be less likely to change their ways, even if it's for the better. They sincerely believe their actions are the only way and are incredibly rigid. The fixed-minded aligns closely with dictators and authoritarian leadership styles.

Growth-minded people believe deeply in change and improvement. This group believes that everyone can improve and develop themselves over time. They align more with the theory that great leaders are "built, not born." The growth mindset accepts life's challenges and understands that knowledge can be gained. These individuals will be more willing to make sacrifices, embrace new thoughts and ideas, and explore new opportunities. They enjoy unfamiliar things and respect the journey of self-development. The growth minders will likely be more mindful and exercise the placebo effect and law of attraction. They are more team-oriented, fearless, and resilient. This group is typical for producing "rags to riches" stories and people who overcome extreme adversity. This mindset is groomed for achieving self-mastery.

Last, those with the victim mindset blame everyone else for their shortcomings. These people firmly believe that the universe is against them and that they were born with bad luck. They believe their life's challenges are deep-rooted and that they are a pure reflection of their ancestors. Individuals with the victim mindset are not willing to develop themselves if it requires relying on others. They are extremely limited people who set low expectations to avoid disappointment and are not likely to accept change. This group aligns with conspiracy theorists and cult-like groups. They make excuses for their underachievements and are notorious procrastinators. The victim minders are often depressed and become manipulators when placed in leadership positions and breed toxic environments. This mindset cannot achieve self-mastery because it goes against the ten pillars.

As you can tell, the ideal mindset is the growth mindset. The good thing is, it doesn't matter if you don't have this mindset today because you can change it. Humans can change how they think, but it requires dedication and persistence. I have worked with people who have developed a long-term growth mindset and those who have developed a short-term one. The critical component of developing a growth mindset is connecting with your purpose. You must want to change and cannot let others negatively influence you. If you create a growth mindset, you can exercise the universal law of attraction and achieve self-mastery. Without it, you will continue to live unfulfilled and not live up to your full potential. Therefore, having the right mindset will give you the foundation that promotes high success and achievement.

Why Positive Mindfulness is Difficult to Gain

One of the main reasons why individuals don't gain positive mindfulness is due to their ingenuine belief in the process. Many people I work with face difficulty buying into the concept of mindfulness. They practice positive thinking only when it's convenient. However, they revert to their old negative thinking when times get tough. Instead of seeing the positive in situations, they point out the negative. For example, in the workplace, if someone gets assigned extra tasks and responsibilities without a pay increase, they tend to look at it as a punishment or as being overworked and taken advantage of. Instead, it could be better viewed as the leader trusting this individual and allowing them to display their abilities. Often, when promotional opportunities arise, the hard-working people who took on extra assignments in stride receive them. However, because they don't genuinely believe in the process of mindfulness, they miss out on many chances. The one thing they attract and manifest can be directly in front of them, but the negative thinking can cloud their vision. To avoid this mistake, you must believe in these concepts wholeheartedly, and they must be embedded into your daily life. Of course, you can't always expect to be happy-go-lucky, but you can train yourself to take a step back and see the positive in many scenarios.

Another common reason positive mindfulness is difficult to gain is because of one's upbringing. Some don't even realize they developed a negative mindset through learned behavior. Growing up in a family with a fixed or victim mindset can contaminate you if left unchecked. These households breed hostile cultures that can continue for generations. Children who grow up in these conditions typically learn the behavior most often displayed. Therefore, by the time they reach adulthood, they tend to repeat the cycle of a wrong mentality. It's natural not to challenge one's upbringing, but if you're now in a position to make a difference, you should. Far too often, I meet people who aren't working towards their dreams because of embedded negative mindsets. They just let life happen and aren't getting after it because it's what they were taught. As the saying goes, "The apple doesn't fall too far from the tree." This is a common issue, but if it sounds familiar, you owe it to your family to be the one to break the curse. You can start by raising awareness among your loved ones and verbalizing that you want to change. Remember, manifesting is speaking things into existence. A great practice is to get your family involved in positive thinking by leading by example. You will see things shift in a better direction over time as long as you stay focused on gaining control of your thoughts.

Mindfulness is also difficult to gain for those who lack emotional intelligence. As you recall, mindfulness is the practice of gaining control and complete awareness of one's thoughts, emotions, etc. Those who lack emotional intelligence struggle to make sound decisions that trigger their emotions. They face difficulty gaining control over their feelings and usually react to situations without thinking. Many would say they respond with their hearts before their minds. Thus, these individuals let their emotional attachments guide them, and when things get tough, they react out of anger, sadness, or depression. Keeping your emotions in check is critical to gaining mindfulness because foolish or hasty decisions get made when stress is involved. At heightened states of anxiety, mindfulness must be in full effect because you will make better choices. I've learned to laugh at high-stress points in my life. (You read that right, yes, I actually laugh.) Some may think I'm crazy, but it works for me. Others may count to five or ten; some count backward and take deep breaths. I've tried it all. The point is that you must recognize when stress presents itself and then take a counteractive measure to deflect it.

How to Achieve Mindfulness

The previous sections helped you explore the wonderful powers of the mind. You learned that mindset is the reality of one's thoughts and beliefs and that mindfulness is the complete awareness of one's thoughts, emotions, or experiences. I want to point out that your mindset is not set in stone; it is changeable. You can change your perspective on life with a bit of practice and good habits. Your mindset is the switch that turns on the light to all your dreams, goals, and ambitions. It's the key or the button that starts the ignition to the vehicle that will take you to your destination. In other words, mindset is everything. Without the right one, you will struggle to achieve self-mastery and set yourself up for continuous failure and disappointment. However, with the right mindset, you can develop mindfulness and control your destiny. You can attract exactly what you want and manifest it as you learn to be optimistic. The following will show you other ways to achieve mindfulness and apply it to your life.

1. **Reject negativity**

   a. You must reject all negativity that comes your way to make room for optimism. Our minds are designed to remain full through a constant exchange of information. Rejecting negativity allows you to make space for positive interactions to get you to the point where the positive outweighs and overpowers the negative. You should steer away from unhealthy conversations and media that will corrupt you. Awareness is vital, as you learned, and you should always be aware of your environment, but engaging in negativity should be avoided.

b. Similar to what you learned in how to raise your limits, rejecting negativity also includes changing your associates. You must remove negative people from your life as much as possible. As you develop yourself, you will want to help others, especially those you lead. But you must bring them into your world without getting sucked into theirs. Negative energy is more contagious than positive energy because it requires less work, and the groups are more prominent. Self-masters are part of the minority, the one percent you hear about. To become a member, you must practice distancing yourself from negativity in all aspects.

2. Take aggressive action

a. Nothing mentioned in this chapter is attainable without taking aggressive action. This step is where many people fall short. This is your life we are talking about, so why not be aggressive in your approach? There is absolutely no point in attracting the things you desire if you aren't willing to put in the work to close the loop. The law of attraction does not work without action because the lack of it creates misalignment. No one achieves high success by sitting around praying and wishing for change. It only makes you a beggar, and as the saying goes, "Beggars can't be choosers."

b. You must be deliberate about your goals and put every effort into reaching them. Those who take aggressive action rarely miss their targets. Taking aggressive action requires passion and persistence. This type of action does not need to be uncontrolled and messy. In fact, you should have a flair and finesse as you navigate your course. The point is that your efforts and energy level should be aggressive, but those looking from the outside should see someone glowing and well-composed.

3. **Focus on your mental health**

a. Mental health challenges are more prevalent in today's society. According to the Centers for Disease Control and Prevention, more than 1 in 5 adults live with a mental illness. Therefore, focusing on your mental health is crucial to gaining mindfulness. If you do not care for your brain, your mind will deteriorate, and you will face hardship in achieving success. You can improve your mental health by scheduling time to engage in activities, hobbies, and vacations to detach from the day-to-day.

b. Maintaining good mental health is equally important as maintaining good physical health. You shouldn't be ashamed to seek counseling or talk to a mentor when necessary. These people can help you understand what you're going through and give you advice. It is also wise to avoid illegal drug use and abusing alcohol because it can destroy your mind and severely cloud your judgment. Why put in so much effort to reach your goals if you don't plan to maintain them? Focusing on your mental health will help you protect your mind.

4. **Find time to be at peace with yourself**

a. You must frequently remove all distractions to be at peace with yourself. Two of my favorite ways to do this are taking a 30-minute walk and spending 15 minutes meditating in the sauna/ steam room. Spending this time with myself helps me gather my thoughts and propels me forward. I've found many solutions to my issues, created business ideas, and discovered answers to tough choices by performing these activities.

b. All it takes is 15 to 30 minutes every other day

to experience significant change by doing this. Spending this time alone is just the amount you need to develop your mindfulness. There are considerable proven health benefits to walking and meditating. However, be careful not to overindulge in this alone time because it can also work against you and lead you into an unproductive state. Stick to this recommendation; you will notice an overall improvement in your mindset, emotions, and reactions.

5. Prioritize your goals

a. It's great to be ambitious, and the self-master is the most ambitious being of all. Nonetheless, you must have order in your ventures. You should not attempt too lofty goals simultaneously because you will wear yourself out. Instead, you must learn to prioritize your goals by understanding your resources and what is essential to achieve first. Exercising your situational awareness will help you improve your prioritizing skills.

b. In today's age, you can choose from many online tools to help prioritize your goals. If you are more of a technical person or want to become one, then online project management tools can help you prioritize and break up your goals by turning them into projects. Knowing the order in which you must handle things will contribute to your mindfulness and keep you performing optimally.

By taking these steps, you can gain complete control of your thoughts and tap into the power of the universal law of attraction. The concepts and techniques mentioned throughout this chapter are logical ways to develop mindfulness. I've learned through personal endeavors, studying others, and researching methods to deliver this information to you based on factual evidence. The human mind is truly capable of the unthinkable. What's vital to remember is that your perception is reality, and how you view yourself will determine your outcomes. To succeed, you must spend each day with a growth mindset, ready to take on all challenges. If your mind is not in top shape and conditioned to perform in the midst of today's storms, you are doing yourself a disservice. Think about this: If you can't control your mind and emotions, how do you expect to lead the extraordinary life you want to live? Let the universe work in your favor, and you can scribe your life's novel.

6

Accountability, The Forgotten Skill

Blame Culture

Throughout my leadership experience, I've learned that pointing the finger at someone else is always the preferred choice for unwarranted outcomes. Too often, I've witnessed people miss targets and blame everyone else involved in the process except for themselves. This issue is one of the primary struggles for leaders, and it is even more prevalent among new ones. Blaming others for mistakes occurs in all environments. You may see it within the home, workplace, educational system, military, and government, basically anywhere you can think of. This phenomenon of blaming others within a hierarchical system is known as "blame culture." Blame culture occurs more frequently in environments where individuals fear the consequences of making mistakes. Instead of being truthful about the root cause of the issues, these people would rather throw others under the bus to save themselves. Think of how many people you know that fit this description. Are you one of them? Not that you would admit it at this point, but if so, don't beat yourself up over it because it's actually easy to fall into this trap.

Blame culture is easy to participate in because passing responsibility on others is triggered by our fight or flight hormone. As you learned earlier, this hormone helps to protect us in stressful situations. Thus, when organizational failures occur, the natural response for leaders is to react defensively instead of taking accountability for their actions. Merriam-Webster defines accountability as *"an obligation or willingness to accept responsibility or to account for one's actions."* The key point here is accepting responsibility. Whether good or bad, leaders must always take responsibility for their contributions and actions toward outcomes. They must understand that they take part in whatever they touch, but no one is perfect, and mistakes will happen. Whether you are a designated leader in your environment or not, you must lead yourself above all. Learning how to lead yourself is what brought you here; it's the core of self-mastery and the basis of what the concept hinges on. This is why I want you to continue this chapter with an open mind and accept that you cannot slack on the Pillar of Accountability. Accountability is equally important as the other self-mastery pillars, but it is harder to achieve because it is the most frequently tested. Understanding blame culture will heighten your awareness and prepare you to learn how to be more accountable. The following is an example of what it looks like.

You're a departmental leader within an organization and assigned to bring on a new service line. Your boss tells you they want you to handle the entire project, from set up to implementation. You believe your job may be on the line if you can't deliver because of previous experiences you've seen. After receiving your instructions, you begin working and gather your team to discuss the details. Throughout your team discussion, you assign roles and outline the objectives to reach your goal. You then put your foot on the gas and begin progressing with the project. As you start working, you realize you may need more time and resources to complete your goal, so you meet your boss for approval. Your boss approves getting you additional resources but is not happy with your request for extra time and believes you can find a way to make the deadline. During your conversation, you could not produce a valid argument for requesting more time, so your boss suggests you stick to the original plan. Over the course of the project, you begin cutting corners and force your team to work overtime hours to meet the deadline. You explain to the team that the "big boss" would not give you the green light for more time. You completed the project on time but burned out your team in the process. Also, the end product is of lower quality than expected, and the service line is not fully operational. When asked about the outcome, you blame the team for not pulling their weight and not working to their full potential. You also explained that you worked extra-long hours and did your best to meet the deadline, but you just didn't have enough time.

Does this scenario sound familiar? Can you point out the root of the issue here and how often blame was placed elsewhere? This example is one of the millions of countless others occurring daily within organizations. This is an organization of blame culture, and the root cause of the issue was the leader's belief that their job was on the line, which led to the blame game. Leaders blaming others instead of taking responsibility for their actions are silent killers. Their negative actions kill the culture, the stakeholders, the customers, and ultimately themselves. In this example, the leader felt threatened but still should have come prepared to the meeting with their boss to seek additional resources and time. A good leader would have built a solid case with valid points for extending the project. They also would not blame their boss for disapproving their project extension request when they mandated their team to work overtime. Last, the leader should not have accused the group of not working to their full potential, knowing they were burned out due to the leader's mistakes. Each of these blaming scenarios was an opportunity for the leader to step up and own their faults. Had they taken accountability, they could have produced better outcomes for all involved. Instead, the team got burned out, and the service line was sub-par. The leader also lost credibility with the team and their boss for not living up to their mistakes.

The example is a pure case of blame culture. One thing led to the next, causing a chain reaction of bad outcomes. As you lead others, it is critical that you create a culture where people can be honest about their mistakes without fearing retaliation. Accomplishing this type of culture requires balance because you'll also want to avoid allowing mistakes to happen more often. You don't want to be taken advantage of, but you also want your team to own their mistakes. To achieve this ideal culture, you must lead by example. Leadership starts at the top, and when your team witnesses you taking accountability, they will do the same. You can also create this culture by making your team aware of your responsibilities as they relate to specific projects. You can keep them aware of your goals and progress, even discussing setbacks and obstacles to show them how to overcome them. Your team will respect this transparency and vulnerability and will follow suit. A recent study by the American Society of Training and Development discovered that teams have a 95% chance of success when the members meet and hold each other accountable. Therefore, while other leaders may allow blame culture, you can lead your team differently, which will be shown by your performance. Over time, the organization can change as others start to see how much your team will stand out. If it is an organization with a blame culture, it will suffer long-term and eventually be forced to change. You can be the very person who can help lead the change as the board of directors or executives begin looking at the departments individually.

Act Like You Own the Place

Over a decade ago, I gained my first authentic ownership experience within the workplace. This valuable lesson has stuck with me ever since and has been one of the most impactful contributions to my leadership style.

While working as a young senior vice president of an account receivables corporation, I was responsible for recruiting and handling operations. This newly formed company had just gone public, and we had secured significant financial backing from investors. My business partner and I had just left a guaranteed job and were on a streak of highly successful years within the same industry. When we took this leap of faith, we were unsure how things would sort out, but we had a wise mentor and advisor who was well-known as a Wall Street shark, so our confidence was sky-high as we entered these new roles. As we started operations, we were given a budget to work within for all start-up costs. These costs included recruitment needs, supplies, equipment, purchasing leads, etc. The first eye-opening moment took place when we started conducting interviews. We were told to keep all staff salaries a few dollars per hour below the market standard and to negotiate deals to get everything else for the bottom dollar. At this moment, my business partner and I felt we had made the wrong decision and had no idea how to make this work.

'When you can
wholly depend on
yourself, you will not
disappoint others
and will put your
all into everything
you're associated
with.'

We believed we were being set up for failure from the beginning and could not fathom how we didn't see this coming. The company we resigned from had a different view and allowed us to offer top dollar for employees, regardless of the industry standard; we also had top-of-the-line software and equipment. This news from our investors was shocking, but we knew we needed to make do with what we had and make the best of the opportunity. After heated discussions with our advisor and numerous meetings about why this was a foolish approach, he made a statement that I would never forget. During one conference, he said, *"This will not work until you treat this like your own money and start acting like you own the place."* This conversation was our ah-ha moment, and from that point, we started what led to record-breaking months, achieving every goal we set out to hit. Nothing could stand in our way, and we made a successful run that would open the doors to what led me here today.

The previous experience was life-changing and instilled an extreme sense of ownership within me. Treating the company like my own made me more financially conscious and ten times more likely to stay within budget. I made more sound decisions by convincing myself that whatever I did had a direct positive or negative impact on my finances. I realized that the resistance was self-induced and that I could better control my outcomes by changing my stance. From that day on, I accepted full responsibility and ownership, which has become one of my best assets.

Before this experience, I burned through operating budgets as if they didn't exist. I had no conception of the organizational bottom lines because I felt they didn't impact me. Many people think the same way. When I changed this thought process, our company began outperforming our peers month after month. It has been the same case in every industry and every position I have assumed since then. This same philosophy can improve your leadership approach and make you a relentless being. Even small business owners become guilty of not taking ownership. This is how they default on loans, fall into severe debt, go bankrupt, and have IRS issues. Therefore, this technique works for everyone serving a position of responsibility and authority. It allows you to lead more passionately and caring as you work within your role. You will be more cautious about hitting your goals, spending wisely, and hiring the right people. If you struggle with ownership or know you can do better, this is a sure way to improve this skill.

The Human in the Mirror

As I work with others in my roles and interact with many different people, I conclude that society is drifting backward. It's almost like accountability doesn't even exist anymore. No one wants to be responsible; everyone wants to take the easy way out and jump on the latest trend, and entitlement is at an all-time high. Okay, maybe I'm exaggerating, but in all seriousness, we, as a people, need to accept our faults. I was raised with the understanding that at the end of each day, I need to be able to look at myself in the mirror and be happy with the fact that I gave it my all. I still hold myself to that standard, but I believe society has made it acceptable to work less hard and expect more. If you're in a leadership position or involved in recruiting talent, I'm sure you've experienced this first-hand. I can name all sorts of actions to support this conclusion, but in general, I believe the impact of COVID-19 exacerbated this new wave of unaccountability. Not accepting responsibility is so common today that these actions trend on social media and get millions of views. In reality, when people don't hold themselves accountable, they take whatever outcome happens. What many don't realize is how damaging this actually is. Not holding yourself accountable prevents you from going the extra length. In all settings, low performance positively correlates to low accountability. In contrast, high performance moves in the same direction as high accountability. It isn't the root cause of performance but a significant contributing factor. The relationship between the two is directly related to progress and results. Therefore, if you want better results, try holding yourself more accountable.

When I teach others about accountability, I remind them that it starts with the individual. You must be able to look into the mirror and know that you can count on yourself above all. Sure, it's terrific and ideal that others can rely on you, but you will never need to worry about that when you put every effort into relying on yourself. When you can wholly depend on yourself, you will not disappoint others and will put your all into everything you're associated with. You can build yourself up to this level by owning your mistakes, being honorable, and being thorough and diligent in your work. The self-master embodies this skill and walks away from tasks confidently, knowing that the outcome is always their best work. They're not perfect, but they try to minimize mistakes, and when they make them, they learn from them and make adjustments in stride. The self-master knows that hiding from mistakes and blaming others prevents them from learning, and since they have a growth mindset, they understand that learning is fuel to their evolution.

You can also get there, but you can't settle for average. Being average is not good enough because it won't get you the life you desire. High achievers don't slack on themselves; they become one with their responsibilities and obsessed with ownership. They reach success by maintaining control through accountability. There's no secret to it; it's just a forgotten skill. Gaining accountability can be improved steadily, but it has a quick impact. So, dive into it. The next opportunity you have, take one small accountable action and record the result. You have to look for it because you can easily miss the chance and resort to your old ways. It may even make you uncomfortable, but this is good because it means you have an opportunity to grow, and that is precisely where you want to be: constantly advancing and moving forward.

Why People Don't Hold Themselves Accountable

People don't hold themselves accountable primarily because they want to protect their self-image. They don't want to lose their respect and be viewed as incompetent. In most cases, their fear of embarrassment is greater than their willingness to learn from their mistakes. Thus, when something tests their knowledge or abilities, they take the first opportunity to escape by passing the blame onto something or someone else. This is typically when the excuses arrive, and these individuals try to justify their actions with every other reason besides the truth. Instead of accepting criticism and feedback, they deflect the target onto something else and hide from the spotlight. We all have been here at some point in our careers, and maybe you're still there now or know someone guilty of this. Trying to protect your self-image this way is not worth it. Most good leaders can see through this tactic; it just makes the person less trustworthy and unreliable and will eventually cause them to be viewed as a low performer. Ironically, they actually ruin their self-image even more when taking this approach. In all my experiences, I've gained more wisdom and increased my self-image by owning my mistakes and receiving feedback rather than shifting the onus elsewhere. I suggest you consider this explanation the next time temptation creeps up to point the finger.

Another common reason people avoid accountability is due to their lack of care. This is a simple answer, but some people just don't care enough. To be fair, it's not realistic to be passionate about everything. However, in your success journey, you will be placed in roles that are simply stepping stones to your goal. Those roles may not be where you want to be, but they are critical to your path. For example, you may be in an entry-level position on a career track to your long-term plan. Or, you may have had to accept a non-related role to your goal but knew it was the best way to get your foot in the door of an organization with the growth potential you're looking for. In both examples, it's easy not to be enthusiastic about the position. Nonetheless, these are the best opportunities to prove yourself. You must care about being accountable, or your goals will suffer. You need to be passionate about the journey, and when you do, you will care about every responsibility you have.

This third reason may not surprise you because it's pretty obvious—many people don't hold themselves accountable because they get used to others picking up their slack. This frequently happens in team settings. Being on teams often allows members to hide behind their star players. They take advantage of this and don't work their best because they know the stars will carry the load, especially when working towards a common goal. The issue can also reveal itself in relationships or anytime more than one person is involved in a task.

Getting caught up in this calamity is effortless, so try to avoid doing it at all costs. Never try taking a "back seat" when you're being counted on to play your part. It's unethical, destructive, and outright disrespectful. Instead, if this temptation creeps up, try putting yourself in the shoes of your teammates. Reverse the role and try understanding how you would feel if someone deceived you into picking up their slack. If you see this happening in your setting, speak up and challenge the offender if you have the authority to. Your focus should be to reach a level where you always contribute your best efforts. Awareness of these common reasons will help you spot and overcome them if applicable.

How to Develop Your Accountability

Accountability encompasses more than just taking responsibility and ownership for one's actions. It embraces the idea that people must follow through on their promises and make every effort to accomplish their tasks. Others should be able to rely on you when you give them your word, but most importantly, you should be able to rely on yourself. Many people fall short in accountability because they don't focus on quality; instead, they just want to get things done. This mentality leaves room for error and causes one to make mistakes. Therefore, as you learned, it opens the door for blame culture, deflection, and an environment where the majority slacks off. Accountability is vital to becoming a self-master, and you must accept that your words and commitments hold value. Thus, the more accountable you are, the more others will value you, and you will value yourself. So, if you want to increase your value, develop your accountability. Here are some additional ways to achieve this.

1. **Understand your strengths and weaknesses**

    a. One of the main reasons people aren't accountable is because they are not fully aware of their strengths and weaknesses. I've seen countless times where people have taken on tasks that they underestimated due to their lack of experience and abilities. There's nothing wrong with taking on challenges to stretch yourself because it leads to growth. However, when doing so, you must understand how your strengths will help you accomplish the task and how your weaknesses may get exploited. Then, you can fully assess how you will reach your goal.

b. Exercise your situational awareness skills to become familiar with your abilities. Doing this lets you evaluate your resources to help you gain an edge by filling a void when your weaknesses may become a barrier. Your responsibilities and tasks will constantly change as you progress; therefore, you will use your strengths differently depending on your objectives. The goal is to continue exercising your awareness so that anything you attempt will get the best version of you.

2. Ensure clear expectations

a. Whether you are a part of a team or working as an individual, it is best to ensure your expectations are clear. You will likely struggle if you don't fully understand your role. Your perception of the objective may also differ from your team members, so it is best to talk it out so everyone is on the same page. Setting clear expectations is a highly effective way to hold people accountable because it limits excuses that can be used later.

b. An ideal way of ensuring clear expectations is by assigning responsibilities in writing. This method works tremendously in partnerships and work settings. Make it a priority to write down and discuss your duties. Don't just passively work on projects without clarifying what others expect from you. If you're leading, do the same for your followers and write what you expect from them until they learn to do it independently.

3. **Rinse and repeat**

a. Everyone wants efficiency, and a significant part of that is knowing when you don't need to reinvent the wheel. As you develop yourself, others will soon recognize you as a subject-matter expert and one they can count on. Remember to record your best wins and understand the formula that went into them. This will help you build your arsenal, and you can apply the same approach when faced with similar tasks.

b. Doing this will help you build confidence and experience because you will exercise your strengths more frequently. The rinse and repeat technique will reduce your chances for error; thus, it can increase your engagement and ownership. This will improve performance because solutions come more naturally with familiarity as you work through your objectives.

4. **Find an accountability partner**

   a. Anyone who knows me knows I firmly believe in keeping plans to myself. In fact, this has served me well throughout my career because I know that all the decisions I've made are mine alone. However, most don't know that I usually have an accountability partner involved in my moves. An accountability partner is a trusted person with whom you discuss your plans and meet routinely to hold you accountable. They will challenge you, call you out when you're slacking, and not allow you to make excuses.

   b. Accountability partners are members of your support system you can continuously tap into. These individuals will help you improve your accountability by keeping you on track and being available for you to bounce ideas off as you sort through your obligations. We will explore this more deeply in the next chapter.

5. **Identify what failure looks like**

   a. You learned to identify the worst outcomes as part of a way to increase your limitations in Chapter 3. Expanding on this by identifying what failure looks like can also help improve your accountability. To do this, think about what would happen if you did not meet the expectations of your role. This exercise is a sure way to improve your ownership because you will learn the vitality of your contributions or lack thereof.

b. Many avoid this technique because they would rather not know how their efforts impact the team. Ignorance is bliss. It is much easier to ignore the reality of responsibilities than to accept that your errors and failures can do more than cause stress. Get familiar with this informational awareness, and it will set you apart from many.

Your relationships depend on your accountability. It is the soil that allows your thoughts, dreams, and ideas to flourish. Those who struggle with it find it hard to be trusted and don't trust their own judgment. Teams and organizations run by leaders who hold themselves and one another accountable are more likely to reach their goals. According to the Association of Talent Development, those who commit to each other have a 65% chance of completing their goal. The best organizations run like well-oiled machines because their leaders can trust that tasks are handled without second-guessing if the work is being done. This level of accountability is the gold standard and where you should ascend. I advise putting your all into your responsibilities and leaving no room for questioning. You will gain more control and feel more deserving of your outcomes. Accountability is a forgotten skill; it is your duty to master it and teach those you care about how to hone it.

7

Support Systems

Pillar of Support

The goal of pursuing self-mastery is to gain complete control over leading and developing yourself to always be at your full potential. However, while you focus on your own growth, it is crucial to understand how others fit into your life. Your life's equation will always be a product of your contributions and support systems. So, it is wise to do your best to embrace them. According to Merriam-Webster, a support system is *"a network of people who provide an individual with practical or emotional support."* Throughout my experience, I've learned that the best support systems are not self-centered; they are a two-way street. In other words, your system helps you while you help your system. This chapter will teach you about critical support systems and their impact on your evolution. Now, let's begin!

The Starting Five Lineup

*"The strength of the team is each individual member.
The strength of each member is the team."*
—Phil Jackson.

Every person should have a starting five lineup of their closest friends to help them navigate life. You can accomplish so much independently, but your strengths are even more multiplied when you have a team. Throughout this book, I've mentioned teams in terms of the groups of people you work with, lead, and associate with. In the *Limitless Capabilities* chapter, I also explained how changing your inner circle can help you expand your limits. Now, it's time to explore this information deeper to learn how developing this power circle can allow you to experience unimaginable victories. There is tremendous strength in numbers. One of the most incredible benefits of pursuing self-mastery is the goal-driven power it produces when these individuals come together as one. Organizing your team can lead to managing an entire empire! However, developing a successful team or company is no simple process. Your mission is to assimilate your starting five lineup of individuals all working towards common goals. I've learned a unique way to conceptualize this. Like a standard basketball team, your team should have the following roles.

The Point Guard: This position is an extension of the coach on the court. They are primarily responsible for setting up the offense and controlling the team's pace. Among these responsibilities, the point guard's primary duty is to continuously pass the ball and create the best opportunities for their teammates to score. By maintaining awareness and a high basketball IQ, the point guard anticipates the defensive strategies and works to maintain possession of the ball within their team.

As it relates to life and assembling your personal team, the point guard is the person who provides the majority of resources. This individual has a clear vision and makes significant connections throughout life to help the team. They are specialists in understanding current trends and opening doors for their teammates to score. On many teams, they are one of the primary leaders and think about high-level priorities. Their mission is to distribute their resources most effectively to reach victory. The point guard is often an investor or someone who can connect the team with the necessary capital expenditures. They usually take on the Chief Executive or Chief Financial Officer positions.

The Shooting Guard: This position is an all-around scorer and often the team's best shooter. They are usually the person the offense revolves around and are the second-best basketball-handlers. The shooting guard takes control of the ball and manages the offensive plays when the point guard needs help. However, their primary responsibility is to score, as they can score from anywhere. They focus on getting open shots and taking advantage of defensive mismatches.

The shooting guard is the team's assassin on your starting five lineup. They can take advantage of all the resources the point guard provides and put them to use best. This person is primarily the team's mastermind and organizes the plans. They also gather resources and build connections alongside the point guard. This individual is typically the go-to person for the team. They handle high-level priorities and manage the day-to-day to ensure the team reaches its goals. In many groups, they are the strategists and assume the Chief Executive or Chief Operating Officer role.

The Small Forward: The small forward is known as the jack of all trades on the basketball court. They are usually taller and stronger than the shooting guard but can also score from nearly anywhere. Besides scoring, they are responsible for getting rebounds and playing defense. The small forward is the best defensive player on many teams because of their skill set, size, and strength. They can also dribble the ball well, which makes them a significant threat.

In your power circle, the small forward will help achieve individual tasks. They are mainly the project managers who ensure each project or business unit succeeds. They lead their own teams and work to facilitate the strategies set forth by the point guard and shooting guard. This individual is primarily out in the field, getting their hands dirty and keeping the team sharp. Being so close to the action, they also help identify threats and disruptions before they impact the team. The shooting guard aligns closely with the Project Director or process improvement positions.

The Power Forward: The power forward is the second-tallest member of the team. Besides height, they are typically stronger and more aggressive than the smaller positions. Their primary responsibility is to rebound and get second-chance opportunities for the team when they miss a basket. The power forward is good at making mid-range shots and scoring near the rim. They notably have less ball handle than the small forward but control the ball by playing with their back to the basket and using their body to push off defenders.

This position is the team's spokesperson and networker. The power forward is excellent at marketing and communications. They support the team by handling the branding strategies and ensuring their customers know them. The power forward is responsible for all public relations and helps keep the team aware of outside engagement opportunities. They are not directly involved in leading, but their efforts significantly give their playmakers the best winning chances. This individual usually assumes the Chief Marketing, Chief Communications Officer, or public relations positions.

The Center: This position is the team's tallest member and usually the strongest. The center plays the closest to the basket and rarely takes shots outside the paint. Their main responsibility is to stop the opposing team from scoring by blocking their shots and contesting anyone who gets close to the rim. They are highly defensive players but can rebound and score easily when they receive a pass because they stay close to the rim.

The center is the team's risk manager. They are responsible for blocking all threats to the team. This person challenges others and protects the team to ensure they remain focused on their goals. They are often well aware and educated on regulatory issues and legalities. They keep their ears to the street to understand industry changes that can impact operations. On many teams, this individual also leads compliance, submits paperwork, and helps the operations leader keep the team organized. The center typically assumes the roles of Legal, Chief Compliance, or risk management positions.

Learning the responsibilities of these positions will help you develop your all-star team. You must aim to identify the role that fits everyone within your circle best, starting with yourself. Once you understand your position, you can evaluate the rest of your team member assignments. Some teams may also consist of individuals assuming multiple positions. For example, your shooting guard and power forward may be the same person, and so forth. Once you learn your roles, your team can begin working to the best of their abilities. Developing your starting five takes time, so you shouldn't be disappointed if you do not have all the positions filled now. Finding five individual members is ideal, but the main priority is to fill the roles. As you develop yourself and work towards mastery, you may discover that your best friends are unwilling to commit to long-term achievement because it's hard work. Therefore, it is not uncommon that you may need to reevaluate your power circle and start networking more to build new relationships with those who share common goals. Always remember that your focus in life is continuous evolution. As you evolve, so should your team, and your starting five lineup will help you win championships.

The Power of Networking

Maybe you're wondering what to do when you're truly alone or realize that your circle doesn't share the same passion as you. Or, perhaps you need to expand your team to reach your starting five lineup. You will likely face one of these challenges and should plan for it. Early in this book, I introduced you to the power of networking. At this point, you should be familiar with some benefits, such as raising your situational awareness and limitations. But successful networking can do so much more for your career. It can help you open doors you may never have had access to. It can also help you build life-long relationships with people who can join your starting five lineup. For me, that was the case. But it didn't come naturally until I unlocked my charisma and developed my networking skillset. You can also do the same with deliberate focus and guidance.

I don't believe in the saying, "It's not what you know; it's who you know." This statement doesn't address the obvious fact that it takes a fearless person with good situational awareness to network successfully. Introducing oneself to a total stranger takes grit and a positive mindset. Some people naturally have this gift, but it's rare. Therefore, most will need to learn how to develop and apply networking skills to get out there and meet the world. I would not be where I am today without meeting others, but networking was not my strong suit in the past. One of my closest friends helped me tap into this skill by sharing his view of my lack of meeting new people. He was naturally gifted at networking and used it to earn massive opportunities. Years ago, he explained that it was all I was missing, and I took those words to heart. That conversation was one of the defining moments that changed my perspective and improved my life. I haven't looked back since and have continued building my network.

Networking is reaching out and selling yourself to unfamiliar people to build relationships. I want to clarify that it is not contacting people to beg for a handout. Doing that is just annoying and will rub others the wrong way. You must share your experiences, abilities, and skills to inform those you want to network with so that you can bring something to the table. The key to networking is understanding that it is a give-and-take relationship. You must be willing to give and express how you can before you should expect to take. Your approach should always be authentic and humbling because people who allow others into their network can usually see through the fakeness. Therefore, your aim should be to build long-term relationships and consistent communication, not just check in occasionally to ask for a favor. If you follow this advice, you can become highly effective at networking.

As I mentioned, some of my most excellent opportunities came from networking. Engaging in the process helps you align with others on the same path.

Think about your goals and what's missing to accomplish them. Often, you may find that you lack the knowledge or resources to move your plans forward. This is where the power of networking kicks in because it can help you fill the gaps. Building relationships with others gives you speed and momentum. You gain the experience of others without having to commit the time. Think about how long it took you to learn your skills. Rather than hiring an expert, consider networking to fill the void. What you can offer may be just what someone else is missing to move their plans forward. Thus, they may be searching for someone with your skills and experience just as much as you are searching for theirs. You will be surprised at how often this occurs. In this case, when these connections are made, they develop into organic bonds that were meant to be. You will then create a synergy of shared resources as you bring your targets together and take them out as a unit. You can develop a vast network of people to help you with anything you need by doing this multiple times. This support system is one of the most impactful ways to accomplish massive goals and success. All it takes is to engage in the process and commit to your evolution through self-mastery to continue increasing your value. The more valuable you are to your network, the more valuable it will be to you. This power creates an actual win-win situation.

Choosing Your Life Partner

Out of all the support systems, one of the most crucial to anyone's success, or lack thereof, is their significant other. The person you choose as your life partner can indirectly impact your focus because they are involved in everything you do. When you learned about gaining mindfulness, you discovered the power of the universal law of attraction and how positive or negative influence becomes a reality. Thus, the role of your life partner is one that you must take extremely seriously because they can make or break you. Your primary focus should be choosing someone who supports your goals and pushes you to evolve continuously. As you strive to reach your career goals, you will have many challenges to overcome. The last thing you want is to allow your partner to become another obstacle in your way. Unfortunately, this happens when one's significant other is unsupportive of their journey. They end up putting unnecessary energy into defending their arguments, and instead of focusing on strategy, their time gets pulled away to plead their case and fight for their dreams. Being in this type of relationship becomes toxic, and you should avoid it at all costs. Of course, there will be arguments and disagreements in relationships, but once you have committed to a goal, your partner should contribute to helping you achieve it.

An ideal life partner should push the other to become great. Their contributions to the relationship should be aligned with their partner's goals. Both individuals must do everything possible to make the required sacrifices for success. While some relationships may involve one highly-ambitious person, others may include both who are go-getters. Therefore, it is essential to understand your dynamic and conversate clearly about your short and long-term goals. You want to identify any conflict between them so you can gameplan and ensure you both accomplish what you want out of life. Clear communication and role acceptance are crucial to a healthy relationship and goal achievement. If you are in a long-term relationship and do not have this understanding, it is wise to establish it, or you will find yourself settling for less to please your partner and avoid arguments. If your relationship is relatively new, or you are still searching for a partner, you should become familiar with having open discussions about your goals. Once you can connect with your partner at this level, you will discover how your path becomes more evident. Then, instead of arguing about WHY you're doing what you're doing, you can talk about HOW your partner can help clear your path or speed up the process. Your relationship can then become fuel to help you drive further ahead. You will have much less resistance and more momentum.

You and your life partner can support one another in many ways. For starters, allowing one the time and space to be productive is one of the most fundamental

'When lone
wolves leave the
pack, they often
don't survive in
the wilderness
and succumb to
the environment
unless they join
or start a new
one.'

contributions you can offer. It is also the one that many couples argue over and struggle with. Hence, discussing your plans can help you understand the time commitment to reach your objective. To gain more support in this area, you must include the time you will spend with your partner in your plans. Another vital contribution to the life partnership is the level of engagement in the goals. Genuinely asking about how things are going, looking for other supporting opportunities, and celebrating small victories can go a long way. Your life partner should be your biggest cheerleader. They should also try to find ways to keep you moving forward, such as motivating, giving you positive affirmations, and recognizing when things aren't progressing. Your partner should be your extra set of eyes when challenges set you back, or you have a decision you are struggling with. The person you choose should also grow with you. You must ensure they are as dedicated to their personal growth as you are, even if they are not nearly as ambitious. If you are in a position to teach them, you must also dedicate your time to helping them learn what will allow them to accomplish their goals.

Life partners should not allow jealousy to get in the way of success. I've witnessed and experienced past relationships where the partner is too jealous to let their significant other interact with the opposite sex. These wishes are unrealistic and unavoidable. We do not live in a world where only one sex exists, so to believe that your partner will not interact with the opposite is foolish. If you experience goal resistance from your partner due to this reasoning, it is a clear red flag. This concern should not get in the way of accomplishing your goals, so if you notice it, you must talk about it. You must expose why it is a concern and navigate it, or it will become a barrier. If any partner allows jealousy to impact their path, they will become unsupportive of one another, leading to resentment. However, jealousy of the opposite sex is not the only jealousy in relationships. There is also the envy of seeing one partner win more than the other. You must identify this issue and disrupt it before it destroys your objectives. Many people let this jealous nature become them; therefore, who you select as a life partner is as critical as the goals you choose to pursue.

Choosing the right partner can help you live a fulfilled life. They will push you to higher levels by supporting you and helping you move with a clear mind. Their support feeds your mindset and keeps you on a course to accomplish your tasks. Not only do they support you mentally, but they can help remove physical barriers to give you the best winning opportunities. The last thing you should want to experience is dealing with your day-to-day industry and relationship challenges, both fighting against your goals. Conversely, your partner should become your teammate, with both of you fighting to win at life. Your aim must be to become a two-headed monster to take on life's obstacles. Therefore, you must evaluate your partner beyond their physical attributes and understand that they will become more than just a part of your life. They will also become a part of your accomplishments. When your partner helps support your goals, they can help you gain the edge you need, but when they don't or inflict resistance, they can adversely impact your success.

Why Some Can't Find the Support They Need

Many people can't find the support they need because they are in the wrong environment. This chapter taught you that building a support system is a selection process. Thus, selecting people who can support you becomes a priority. Think of it this way: you can't catch high-quality fish in polluted waters. Fishermen understand this, and the concept is the same. You must put yourself in the right environment to capture your preferred fish. You can always find a diamond in the rough, but why put yourself through that rigorous process when you can dramatically increase your chances by being in the right place? Many people fall short in this area because they lack situational awareness. They can't find the right support system and end up meeting the wrong people coincidently. Hence, as you become more familiar with the Pillar of Situational Awareness, you will gain all the required knowledge to avoid this mistake. Now that you've reached this chapter, you can see how beneficial it becomes to study and learn these earlier steps. If you struggle with choosing the right people, go back and review what you learned in Chapter 1 to understand how to assess your surroundings.

I touched on the following reason early in this chapter: people fear networking. This was my struggle as a young leader, and it is expected. Reaching out to someone you don't know is uncomfortable, but you must continue putting in the effort until it becomes comfortable. Networking is one of those skills that improves with consistency. However, many who can't build their support system face difficulty getting started. They fear being turned down and told "no." This fear is similar to dating and searching for a mate—rejection is inevitable. Understandably, not everyone will be okay with helping you reach your goals and become part of your network. So, you must accept that you will experience rejection and get comfortable with it. As explained previously, the focus is to prepare yourself to meet others by learning your skills and what you can offer your support system. You must also focus on the previous steps and concepts you learned in Chapter 4 by becoming fearless. Fearlessness is one of the most impactful attributes toward expanding your network.

Another common reason people don't get the support they need is because they believe they can do it all alone. These individuals don't value working with others because of past negative experiences or false information about networking. This leads to becoming egocentric. They believe others will not have their best interests in mind, so they prefer to become lone wolves. While this approach is sometimes ideal, it can slow down progress and cause one to experience unnecessary barriers. Becoming a self-master does not mean becoming self-centered. There is a clear difference between the two. Self-centered people focus on themselves at the expense of others. In comparison, self-masters concentrate on bettering themselves to work effectively with everyone they encounter. They have absolute control over themselves, and as a result, they attract like-minded people who want to support and advance together. Wolves travel in packs to hunt more efficiently, take on bigger prey, and eat together. When lone wolves leave the pack, they often don't survive in the wilderness and succumb to the environment unless they join or start a new one. Nonetheless, we must adopt the same mentality to live prosperously.

How to Develop Your Support System

Building a stable support system can help propel your career and allow you to accomplish more in shorter periods. Other benefits include having someone to collaborate with who can complement your skills and experience and someone to keep you on track by reassuring and challenging you to improve when needed. The most impactful reason you should develop your support system is to gain the ability to deploy multiple resources at one target—an army fighting together is more powerful than one soldier fighting alone. By selecting the right people, you can multiply your opportunities and gain knowledge faster than learning independently. I prioritize developing my support system and staying engaged with its members for these reasons. Many of my highest achievements were sparked through my support system. Whether it was from a general conversation about my goals, someone writing a letter of recommendation, or directly opening a door, I am proud to say that members of my support system have contributed to my success. And that's the beauty of building one, so you can access a flowing river of resources and cast into it at any moment. You've already learned many ways to develop your support system; now, let's explore a few more.

1. **Pursue higher level education**

    a. This typical nonsense that education is overrated is untrue. Many people feel that pursuing higher education isn't worth it because they don't take advantage of the whole experience. The people who attended college and feel this way are due to them only going for the knowledge and degree. Often, they spread this negativity because they don't know how to put their credentials to use. I built endless bonds with my colleagues in my educational journey, and as an alumni, my professors continue to open doors for me by connecting me with their network.

    b. Pursuing higher level education offers many association opportunities. It provides the chance to connect directly with individuals who share similar paths and goals. There are no ulterior motives to look out for because you share and overcome the same obstacles. These opportunities only occur a few times in one's lifetime, so they are rare. Therefore, when you view education as more than credentials, you can unlock an overabundance of networking experiences.

2. **Ask for a connection**

    a. It may seem like common sense, but doing this was unorthodox for me. As you build your network, asking for a connection is a good practice. A simple referral can connect you with someone who may change your life. Yes, it seems like a sales approach because it is. Instead, you are selling yourself and what you can offer.

b. One of my mentors suggested that I start doing this, and it has become one of my favorite ways to meet people. Doing this will make you uncomfortable initially, but it will become more comfortable with practice. Focus on being authentic and trustworthy; you'll be surprised at how willingly your associates will give you a referral.

3. Give and receive

a. The universal law of attraction can benefit you in numerous ways. Giving does not always need to mean monetarily. I've learned that sharing my knowledge to help someone overcome a barrier or find a solution to a life challenge is much more valuable than giving them money, and it comes back tenfold. Being available to your network members and others without expecting anything in return is a sure way to receive good karma.

b. Look for ways to help people and become a mentor as you develop yourself. Giving your time to teach others and seeking opportunities to guide those who look up to you can benefit society. Your personal support system will expand as you become supportive of others in need. It will all catch up to you, and you will receive the recognition you deserve.

4. **Learn your elevator pitch**

   a. You should realize by now that building your support system involves constant communication. Depending on where you are in your career, a significant amount of your networking will be through reaching up to individuals who may be in positions you strive to reach. This is normal, but they may have their guard up at times, so your approach and opening statement will be vital. Therefore, you must create an effective elevator pitch and rehearse it frequently.

   b. Some of the best elevator pitches are charismatic. They are brief and describe who you are and what you do. You must be able to express your most valuable skills and objectives in just a few sentences. These pitches should grab the attention of the person you are speaking with, keep them engaged, and prompt them to ask for your contact information. Public events and the occasional elevator ride are the perfect time to use them. You never know who you will bump into in an elevator. Be prepared to initiate these conversations, but if you're on the receiving end, do not forget to ask about them.

5. Get involved in the community

    a. Search for opportunities to get involved in your community. Many communities nowadays have associations or some way to interact with their neighbors. Engaging in your direct community is an excellent way to build your support group because you all share typical desires to keep the community prosperous and intact.

    b. Getting out and meeting your neighbors is an easy way to start your networking journey. They are within your proximity, and you will not need to look far to meet people. This is an organic way to network and is very beneficial. Sometimes, your neighbors can become your closest friends.

Interactions are inevitable, so why not make the best of them? Those who dedicate the effort toward building their support systems will receive more support. There's no secret formula to it. Often, we get too involved in our personal experiences to realize that humans were meant to mingle, associate, and break bread with one another. This is not to say that you should go around befriending everyone because, let's face it, not everyone wants to share what they have, let alone give you an opportunity. Some people are just unapproachable or simply want to take you out. As you learned in previous chapters, humans were also designed to compete with one another. However, you already know how to handle competition, as you recall from Chapter 4. Therefore, that leaves the remaining group to become your potential supporters.

8

Time is of the Essence

The Pillar of Timeliness

Knowing how time relates to your daily activities is essential for becoming a self-master. Those who ignore it will find their days pass by, wondering how they still face the same struggles or perhaps are worse off than they were years ago. In contrast, those who embrace time will discover that they can progress and will try to gain control of their time and make better use of it. Time is the one unstoppable constant. It continues regardless of the inventions we create and what we do. However, there are many things we can do to change how it impacts us. According to the Cambridge Dictionary, timeliness is *"the fact or quality of happening at the best possible time or at the right time."* In other words, it means to align with time to become more productive. Self-masters pay close attention to time and respect its power. In return, they gain positive outcomes and life advantages. Attaining the Pillar of Timeliness is another essential element of self-mastery. First, you must understand time's influence on humankind, and then you can learn how gaining timeliness can improve your lifestyle.

Chronophobia and Impatience

Have you ever felt like things were taking too long to manifest? Or maybe you feel like life is just moving too fast at times? These concerns are two opposite extremes people face when setting goals and dealing with time. They are common issues that can drastically change one's pursuit of developing plans. Time itself can become a destroyer of dreams and aspirations if you let it. Many unconsciously allow time to negatively impact their decisions and fall victim to chronophobia and impatience. Both are equally detrimental to your psychological state and must be controlled to move forward in your evolution. Failure to do so can take you down a rabbit hole of doubt and underachievement.

Chronophobia is the extreme fear of losing time. People who experience this feel like time is moving too fast, and they are running out of it. This phobia causes intense anxiety and affects one's behavior. Some who deal with chronophobia avoid making long-term plans and setting goals because they genuinely believe they will not live to experience them. Others engage in hazardous behavior and challenge death because they feel their life is meaningless. Either way, this condition does not allow one to dream big and attempt anything that involves commitment. Unfortunately, this fear is more prevalent among the aging population, low income, and those with disabilities and illnesses. Nonetheless, other groups can experience it, like those who have witnessed or faced traumatic situations. Chronophobia causes anxiety-like symptoms, and many who face it suffer from severe depression, insomnia, alcoholism, or drug abuse in many cases. These individuals live as if death is always around the corner.

Impatience is on the other end of the spectrum. It is the feeling of restlessness and things taking too long. Impatience is far more common than chronophobia and is even more impactful in today's Digital Age. Individuals are becoming less patient and expect instant gratification due to technology. A recent study discovered that people can no longer last more than 10 minutes without checking their cell phones, and 50% of people no longer wait on hold for more than one minute. The patience of humankind is trending downward with no sign of it changing course. Think about all the simple things that require patience—sitting at a traffic light, cooking a meal, waiting in line at a shopping center, etc. Our patience is tested daily, and many people fail at it. The main concern is not the impatience of these minor things; it's the lack of patience when setting goals. Severe impatience can lead to goal paralysis. Those who struggle with exercising patience on little tasks are more likely to display the same behavior with larger ones. Like chronophobia, they also experience anxiety-like symptoms that are exacerbated as time increases. Many severe cases of impatience cause individuals to give up on their dreams because they seem too far away.

'You must learn
how much your
time means to you
and what it will
cost you to waste
it.'

They don't have the willpower to strive for anything that will take time.

Chronophobia and impatience may seem reasonable to some. Many argue that both are natural responses, and to a certain degree, they are. However, they become significant barriers when we let them stop us from being productive members of society. They can negatively affect how you function and prevent you from evolving. In severe cases, they can cause you to go backward until you overcome it or self-destruct. As you move throughout this book, you gain the tools to overcome both issues. Two of the most effective ways to overcome chronophobia and impatience are by applying mindfulness and fearlessness. Exercising mindfulness will guide you to understand how much of your future is actually in your control. Using the techniques, you will stay focused on your goals and know you can achieve them because your perception is reality. Fearlessness will help you deal with the adverse impact of time head-on and keep you ahead of your fears. Whether you fear time moving too fast or wish it would speed up, you will be better prepared to overcome both by becoming a self-master.

Believe it or not, fearing time passing or not having enough of it does not have to impact you negatively. One of the beauties of mindfulness is that you can flip chronophobia and impatience around to work in your favor. I've learned this skill, allowing me to attack my goals relentlessly. By helping my mind to accept that time will pass regardless of what I do, I plan my goals to achieve them as quickly as possible. You may recall me saying, *"Where the mind goes, the body will follow."* in Chapter 1. Well, that's how it's done and how you can train your mind to deal with time. You must assess your situation and develop your plan, knowing you will not let anything stop you from reaching your goals. I've worked on self-mastery for so long that I fully believe I can achieve any goal I pursue. Therefore, I allow the passing of time to push me harder because I believe in my abilities and want to hurry up and reach my target. This level of impatience becomes a positive influence and fuels my evolution. I am no different from anyone; my background was rough, as you learned. Hence, you can also develop this willpower and persistence. By the end of this chapter, you will learn how to respect and effectively use time.

The Value of Time

"Time is free, but it's priceless. You can't own it, but you can use it. You can't keep it, but you can spend it. Once you've lost it you can never get it back."
—Harvey MacKay.

Time is an irreversible progression of infinite events into the future. It is the only commodity that we cannot create or destroy. Some argue that time is not a commodity because it is an intangible source. But we trade and exchange our time daily. We exchange our time for money by receiving an hourly wage. We trade it for moments with our loved ones by attending events and gatherings. However, we also waste time by engaging in unproductivity. The latter is one of the most common reasons some are successful, and others aren't. People are most likely to waste things when they don't understand their value. Consider how wasteful children are. A child will break their toys, spit out food they don't like, and ruin just about anything they are allowed to until they learn to value and cherish things. The concept is the same; no matter how much we age, humans will care better for what is most valuable to them. For this reason, I want to help you learn a deeper meaning of time and how others view it.

Finding the right balance between time and income should be your focal point when considering time.

There is no sense in working 24 hours per day, seven days a week, regardless of the pay rate, because there would be no time to do anything else. It leaves no time to enjoy the income outside of the workday. In contrast, having all the time in the world but no monetary gain is a formula for disaster because you cannot live without income to pay for the bare essentials. Both examples aren't ideal because having all of one and none of the other creates an imbalance of unhappiness and unlivable circumstances. Instead, your plan should be to balance your time appropriately to gain the revenue you want while having the time to enjoy it. The wealthy have this figured out, as they create sources of income that generate revenue without them physically spending their time. They can multiply their time through other means and, as a result, have more time for leisure activities. It is possible to get there, but it takes precise planning, commitment, and time management. This group understands that what they do with their time allows them to maintain and create more wealth. Their mindset is in constant harmony with this relationship.

You must learn how much your time means to you and what it will cost you to waste it. Once identified, wasting time becomes anything that causes you to be unproductive. Make sure to distinguish investing time from unproductivity. Investing your time involves doing things now that will benefit you in the future. Some would categorize this only as goal planning, but other examples include taking mental breaks like doing hobbies, watching television, going out on a date, etc.

These are time investments because they help keep your mind sharp by allowing you to step away from your day-to-day work. This mindfulness technique you learned in Chapter 5 is an excellent way to invest your time for later productivity. Of course, the most beneficial form of using your time should always be directly productive. An ideal balance of splitting it is between 70/30 and 80/20, with the lion's share going toward your explicit action.

A wise approach to truly understanding your value of time is by calculating your current daily net revenue and comparing it to your overall goal. Here's an example of someone making an annual net revenue of $100,000 with an overall goal of $500,000. This calculation would look like this:

» $100,000 (Annual net revenue)/365 = $274 (Daily net revenue)

» $500,000 (Net revenue goal)/365 = $1370 (Daily revenue goal)

By taking these daily revenue amounts and dividing them by 24 hours, this example shows that their current hourly value is eleven dollars. However, their hourly goal is fifty-seven dollars. There is a difference of forty-six dollars per hour that they will need to develop a plan for. These hourly amounts represent the current value of time, which means that this individual would impact their revenue by eleven dollars per hour by becoming less productive. Their time value increases even more as they focus on reaching their overall goal. This exercise is a significant way to make time-based decisions and to help you assess what you categorize as a time-waster. You will find yourself wasting less time and spending more time being productive by identifying your personal value of time. The following section will explain how to handle your time effectively.

Time-Management

We're all unique in many ways. We have different beliefs, dreams, goals, and wishes. We work within various industries and come from different walks of life. That said, we all share time, a common dominator of humankind. No one receives more than 24 hours in a single day. You can't add or subtract from it, but you can waste it, as you previously learned. Therefore, what we do with our time and how we manage it is the differentiating factor of success. How you spend your day directly correlates to how much you can accomplish. It's such a simple formula that many people discount the significance of structuring their day. Time management should always be at the forefront of your thoughts. Too many people just "show up" and expect things to happen magically. But just showing up without a daily plan will only take you so far because you're not working towards anything. When people consistently "show up" to the gym without a plan, they get results but nothing close to their dream goal. This approach produces mediocrity and average results. You're aiming for greatness, and great people do extraordinary things. They pay attention to extreme detail, which separates them from the crowd.

Time management helps you organize your day to increase production. It is a system of ensuring you dedicate the required time to complete what you want.

By working on this skill, you will develop daily habits and routines that will keep you on target. Some people can do much more in a day than others because they are more disciplined. Developing time management skills is a choice, and many people choose against it. Well, I am here to tell you that you can multiply your wins exponentially by improving your time management! I recommend working with a schedule and putting everything you want to accomplish on your calendar. There are many online tools available that can help you schedule and organize your day. Find one that works for you, preferably one that sends reminders and alerts to your smartphone. By blocking your time, you gain control of your day instead of letting the day control you. Through years of practice, these habits will become so engrained in your DNA that your time management will carry you into the future. In a world of chaos and uncertainty, having some order to your day might be just what you need.

Learning this skill has been a key to my success. It's gotten me through my undergrad, graduate school, and doctoral studies, all while running a small business, working full-time, serving in the military part-time, engaging with my family, and maintaining an exercise regimen. What's even more interesting is that each activity received my undivided attention and energy because of my dedication to time management. It allows me to focus solely on the task at hand because I fully respect each activity that reaches my schedule, and those involved also appreciate it. Becoming disciplined helped me to learn how to prioritize, and because of it, I know that if I schedule it, it's critical to me, and I will get to it. You're capable of doing the same. For some, it may take more work than others, but it's achievable. I love developing my time management because it's a work in progress and helps me plan my day-to-day and year-to-year goals. By starting small, you can become familiar with the routines that will eventually become habits. These habits will help you evolve, and you will continue to raise the bar by setting long-term goals on a schedule. If not, you are only robbing yourself of the maximum potential and will continue running aimlessly. Developing time management will allow you to achieve more with more efficiency. Trust me, with some practice and consistency, you can reap the benefits of a more peaceful and organized day.

Why People Don't Gain Timeliness

One common reason people don't gain timeliness is because they lack discipline. They don't want to relinquish their old habits and commit to structure. In the previous section, you recall that discipline is a crucial element of time management. Without it, one would only make plans and continue failing to follow through. Unfortunately, discipline is fading away in today's society. Following orders, even if they're your own, is no longer "trendy" anymore, and being disciplined is cliché. Therefore, it becomes challenging for things to happen at the right time because without following a plan, they happen unintentionally. Being calculated is much more rewarding than living in a continuous cycle of the unknown. Surprises are fun until they're not. Nothing is exciting about going day to day without looking forward to anything. The simple act of marking things off your to-do list is good for your mental health. It releases endorphins, which boost your mood and relieve stress. By gaining discipline, you can develop time management skills and take control of your outcomes. However, if you lack discipline, it will take time to overcome. A good exercise I teach others to develop their discipline is to try breaking one bad habit at a time. They first learn to identify it, then see how long they can do without it. The longer they avoid the habit, the less power it has over them, and then they gain control, only engaging in the activity at will. This technique has worked for me many times and is an excellent strategy to learn the discipline to help you gain timeliness.

Lack of accountability is another barrier to gaining timeliness. It is closely associated with the lack of discipline mentioned previously. Those who struggle with being accountable to others often do the same to themselves. These individuals avoid taking ownership and responsibility for their actions, so the thought of owning their schedule is foreign to them. They could care less about being punctual and overachieving and would instead do the bare minimum, even if it means low standards. Lack of accountability destroys timeliness because it prevents individuals from accepting that they must complete daily tasks to grow. They prefer to roll with the punches and not answer to themselves or anyone else. Do you know of someone who is chronically late for everything? This is a clear sign of someone who lacks accountability. Sure, they will always find an excuse for their behavior, but it is a glaring sign of unaccountability. This level of it significantly impacts timeliness and holds them back. Nonetheless, it pays to identify this issue if it applies to you or someone you know because you have the tools to overcome it. Referencing back to the accountability chapter provides all the knowledge to overcome this barrier. Share what you learned, and use it if needed.

Some people are just poor planners. If the plan

doesn't make sense to accomplish the task, it will lead to inefficiencies. Putting time and effort into a terrible plan is a significant time waster and can cause other unwanted issues, like demotivation and stress. This is an area that requires knowledge and experience. Planning skills are necessary to achieve timeliness, and those who struggle with it must engage in strategy development learning. Of course, there is no perfect way to complete any objective, but there are alternate ways that are more ideal than others. Poor planning is avoidable with collaboration and tapping into one's support system. Working with a team can help you see flaws in your plan and allow you to improve it. Proper planning is the roadmap to help you reach your destinations. Lack of it can take you down a dirt road into a ditch.

How to Achieve Timeliness

Timeliness is more than being punctual. It's the ability to make the best use of your time to accomplish your goals more efficiently. It is about understanding how time relates to your life so you can be more productive and avoid wasting it. To continue evolving, you must respect the time you have and commit to your development. The previous sections offered an abundance of examples and knowledge to help expand your awareness of timeliness. By assessing your time value, you can make better decisions about how you wish to spend it. Always remember that those with better control of their day can achieve more because they can fit in more things within 24 hours. If you genuinely want to reach beyond your dreams, you must gain these skills and apply them to your lifestyle. Let's review some additional steps to achieve timeliness.

1. **Minimize your screen time**

    a. Early in this book, you learned that the global average social media time is nearly two and a half hours daily. Well, what's even more alarming is that the average total screen time is 6 hours and 58 minutes—Talk about a waste of time. Americans are even more guilty, with their total time at 7 hours and 4 minutes! Screen time describes any internet-connected device: smartphones, tablets, televisions, computers, and video games. Think about all that can be accomplished with that much time each day to focus on productivity. If people even dedicated a fraction of that time, there could be more beneficial contributions to society.

b. Screen time is becoming a plague, and we must regain control. I'm not suggesting that you eliminate the devices altogether because, as you know, internet-based technology has benefits, as I mentioned in other chapters. However, the harmful use of screen time is the primary concern. Screen time can harm your development when you find yourself aimlessly browsing and putting your time into it without benefit. Using devices to be productive, such as doing research, education, or anything that can help you achieve your goals, is not what I'm referring to here. You must minimize your bad screen time by using it positively or disconnecting from it to work on your goals. You can easily exchange this time with productivity by knowing how it impacts you.

2. Don't compare your time to others

a. Comparing your timeline to others is a recipe for disaster. You don't know what the other individual has done to get where they are, and your time is YOUR time. Everyone's situation is different and will move at a different speed. Your goal is not to try to keep up with others but to put maximum effort into your plans and continue outdoing yourself. Some things require time and energy; depending on where you start, it can take much longer or happen faster than others. This is nothing to stress over, so don't let it bring you down. If you focus and continue reaching your benchmarks, you will complete your mission. The question is, will you slow yourself down by wasting time dwelling on your jealousy?

b. Did you know that the average age of a CEO in the S&P 500 is now 58 years old? The S&P 500 represents the world's largest companies by market cap. Looking at this statistic should put things into perspective and help you realize that there is no age limit to massive success. When people compare their time to others, it causes them to lose focus and motivation. Be aware of your time, but do not allow the pressure to cause you to break down. Instead, focus on doing your best with your time and continue chipping away at your tasks. As you work on your self-mastery, you will perform better and become more efficient, even though you may not be where you want momentarily.

3. **Exercise your patience**

a. You recall that impatience can become a chronic condition that can cause severe anxiety and goal paralysis. However, your patience can increase by exercising it. Patience is a combination of your mindset and willpower. Therefore, mindfulness helps tremendously, but it will also take rigid discipline to improve this skill. Like our bodies, we can increase our patience by practicing it one activity at a time. It helps to start with minor exercises before going for more extensive tests of your patience—look for opportunities to engage in this process. Some examples include letting others go ahead of you in line, ignoring your phone notifications for some time, responding to emails at specific times, and walking short distances instead of driving your car. These are all ways you can exercise your patience. Don't think this is a waste of time, but rather an investment in your development.

b. Delaying instant gratification by ignoring your phone notifications and responding to emails at specific times will pay dividends. In the Digital Age, it is essential for you to own your devices and not let them own you. Your patience will be tested as you move along your path. The higher your aim, the more your patience is required. Practicing patience on the small things will make you more equipped to manage your big goals.

4. Create good habits

a. Routines become habits, and habits become lifestyles. Good habits will get you past obstacles and guide you to the finish line. Establishing them is vital to your time management skills. They will allow you to plan more precisely. To create habits, you must do routine things for weeks and sometimes months. The old saying that it takes 21 days to form a new habit is a myth. There is no set time that it takes; it all depends on the individual. Developing a new habit takes as long as it takes you to perform the activity unconsciously. The most challenging part for many is to get started, so don't spend time procrastinating; move forward!

b. Bad habits must be eliminated to make room for good ones. Clearing your mental space from bad habits will offer you more real estate to build your new routines. Therefore, removing negative patterns from your life is equally essential as focusing on creating positive ones. An excellent way to achieve this is by changing your environment and eliminating toxic people from your life. Think about what you want to achieve and make it your priority.

5. Learn how to delegate

a. I've met many leaders who struggle with busy work and take on too many tasks. There is a fine line between delegating and dumping your work onto someone. Proper delegating is when leaders assign specific tasks to others so they can focus on higher-level priorities. Those tasks are critical to the long-term plan and keep the project progressing. However, when leaders notice that they have more important matters that require their attention, they must delegate. You must always try to work to your highest ability unless there is a specific reason you need to handle minor tasks, like training someone or ensuring you master the responsibility before passing it on.

b. Delegating will help you achieve your goals faster. It will allow you to spare your time to continue steering the ship. As the captain of your destiny, you must keep your eyes on your target and ensure you don't crash. Spending too much time on the lower level will cause you to miss opportunities and set you back. As you continue developing yourself, your team should follow your example. Creating this culture among your group will ensure everyone works within their scope and everyone's time will be appropriately allocated.

Each day is another chance to get closer to where you want to be. The choice is yours to either waste time or use it to your advantage. Everything mentioned in this chapter can help you gain control of your time and put you in a position to be more productive than you were yesterday. You don't need to spend every minute of your day working, but there are things you must do each day to stay on track and improve your efficiency. Gaining timeliness will allow you to hit your targets faster, with more accuracy and power. You will move with greater velocity while affording you time to enjoy your life. Remember that what you highly value will be highly favored. This is your time, and it is of the essence.

9

Execute or be Executed

Newton's Third Law of Motion

"To every action there is always an equal and opposite or contrary, reaction."
—Sir Issac Newton.

Nothing in this world accelerates without action; it's a scientific fact. Newton's third law of motion describes the law of action and reaction. In physics, this relationship between force and action explains how objects apply equal and opposite forces to one another to maintain balance. When one object exerts more force on the other, it causes the object with the greater force to accelerate. An easily understandable example is imagining someone sitting in a chair. When the person sits still, the chair and the floor apply equal force to the individual, causing balance, also known as equilibrium. However, to get up from the chair, the individual must push down with more force, usually with their feet pushing down to the floor. Therefore, the person can accelerate upwards by applying more opposite force than what is being acted upon them. This basic physics example describes Newtown's third law of motion at work. It is also the fundamental concept I use to explain how the relationship between force and action applies to personal goals. For every action you take, there will always be an opposing force.

You learned early on that exercising situational

awareness should be your first step toward self-mastery. Each pillar plays a unique and vital role in your evolution, but the driving force lies in executing. According to Merriam-Webster, to execute means *"to carry (something) out fully: to put (something) completely into effect."* As I relate to my personal experiences of being an executor, I define execution as *the act of applying relentless force to accomplish an objective.* In other words, it means getting the job done! Reflecting on Newton's third law of motion, you will realize that things don't just happen. Nothing moves without an opposite force acting upon it. Targets don't magically hit themselves, and achievements don't fall out of the sky. All plans require greater acting force than their opposing force, or they will fail! Therefore, people who sit around and do nothing will gain nothing because they aren't applying pressure to anything. On the contrary, those who execute will become highly successful through consistent action. In your journey, you must plan to put relentless force into everything you do. By letting your mindset guide you, you should always be prepared to follow every plan with precise action. Doing so will accelerate you from one goal to the next, allowing you to take on every opportunity that comes your way.

Becoming familiar with opposing forces to goals is beneficial, as they come in many forms. These opposing forces are best understood by sorting them into physical, psychological, and environmental categories. *Physical opposing forces are tangible barriers to one's goal.* Some examples include lack of capital, material resources, and competition. They are best overcome by proper planning and honing in on your situational awareness skills to conduct a SWOT analysis. It would also help to tap into your support system and seek assistance from those who can have your back. *Psychological opposing forces are the mental obstacles toward reaching one's goal.* These barriers are typically self-inflicted issues that prevent one from moving forward. Some examples are doubt, fear, lack of experience or ability, and one of the most threatening, procrastination. Overcoming these concerns requires a combination of techniques from each self-mastery pillar. Depending on your specific psychological struggle, some methods may be used more than others. We'll explore the latter example more in-depth in the following section. The last category is environmental challenges. *Environmental opposing forces are the obstacles that hinder one's goal achievement due to their surroundings.* These challenging forces may include an unsupportive environment, a hostile culture, and industry/local regulation. Situational awareness skills are at the forefront of disrupting these concerns. However, exemplary leadership and accountability techniques will help those more culturally specific barriers.

The point of sharing the opposing forces with you is to help you identify what stands in your way of success. Whatever it is, it will fall under one of the three mentioned categories. Therefore, your prerogative is to learn your goal barriers to plan your attack. These opposing forces are your enemy and should be treated as such. You must apply more direct pressure than they exert upon you to defeat them. The law of motion will work in your favor when you do this. However, it will also work against you when you don't. Goal barriers knock us down when their force is more substantial than ours. They also keep us in equilibrium when their strength is equal and we don't progress. Many call this living in the "rat race" or "running on a hamster wheel." Nonetheless, you can accelerate far beyond your goals by exerting much more force than your opposition. When you do this, you will reach further than you ever imagined, so you must continue to expand your mind and develop your limitless capabilities, as described in earlier chapters. As you continue to create your goals, allowing this natural law to work in your favor becomes advantageous.

Procrastinating Will Kill Your Dreams

How often have you told yourself, "I'll get to it later," or "I'll work on this when it's the right time"? We've all been there; if you haven't, you're already moving in the right direction. Speaking for the majority, I can recall countless times when I've made similar statements before realizing I was doing myself harm. Many don't understand the damage caused by procrastinating. Procrastinating is a form of self-sabotage and is a psychological opposing force to goal-setting. As mentioned previously, in my experience of working with leaders, it is one of the most threatening psychological challenges they face. Procrastinating is the act of putting things off. In many cases, people who procrastinate are guilty of making excuses for not getting things started or completed. They find every reason to delay working on their goals. I've heard every excuse in the book and have told myself a lot of them in the past. One of the most common excuses for procrastinating is related to timing. People often look for the "right time" to move forward. While there is typically an ideal time to do certain things, when it comes to getting started on your goals, the "right time" to take action is always NOW! When people delay making progress, it becomes a time waster. More often than not, postponing things for days turns weeks into months and months into years.

Henceforth, there will never be a perfect time to begin your plan, so you must focus on executing and letting your actions outweigh your excuses.

Individuals choose to procrastinate for several reasons. First, it allows them to do one less thing today. In a world filled with so many distractions, it's easy to let time slip away. When they finally think about what they should work on, they're exhausted, and the day has passed. Second, procrastinating gives these individuals a chance to avoid fear. Some people know what they want to accomplish but are afraid to face the reality of the responsibility. Therefore, they end up talking themselves out of progress because they want to stay in their comfort zone. Third, individuals choose to procrastinate due to negative influences. They speak to the wrong people about their plans or let the internet cloud their thoughts. Some even do both, but this happens when they lack good judgment. They will spend time convincing themselves that they are making the right decision but then let non-stakeholders change their stance. Does any of this sound familiar? There are more explanations for why people procrastinate, but the ones I've mentioned are widespread. At some point throughout my career, I've been an offender of each, but I have mastered overcoming them through execution. The purpose of this section is to help you develop this ability.

Delaying your plans will kill your dreams, and you will lose more motivation each time you allow procrastination to set in. Whenever you continuously

'Those who
become high
executors gain
more income and
live better lives
because they
perform above
average each and
every day.'

put off what you want to achieve, you reduce the value of your goals by piling more and more excuses on top of them. When the dust settles, and you think you may be ready to move forward, your goal is barely recognizable. In many cases, the amount of energy to apply now is diminished because it is challenging to match the adrenaline as when the plan was first envisioned. Typically, when someone first envisions a project, they are at their highest level of execution. Therefore, there is a short window to react while in peak performance, and the longer this time extends before taking action, the less effort they will apply. Simply waiting and doing nothing can ultimately reduce the success level of your opportunities. This is not to say you should rush into things unprepared, but if you settle on an idea, you should begin your first steps immediately: developing your plan and identifying your timeline. Creating unnecessary delays should never become a part of your formula.

Fighting against procrastination is all about staying in tune with your purpose. Even down to the minor tasks, when you keep your "why" in mind, you will be less likely to procrastinate because you know that each progression benefits you. However, procrastination attacks on all fronts. Some people face it in the workplace, at home, and practically anywhere that requires them to take action. This omnipresent attack makes it conducive to creating one main focal point to overcome it: YOUR "WHY." This approach has led me to become a reliable executor. Over time, I have managed to rid myself of procrastination completely. Doing so has made me a highly reliable executor because I do not hesitate and waste unnecessary time. You, too, can accomplish the same skills. By focusing on your purpose, you can easily apply the tools required to defeat procrastinating, like timeliness, accountability, fearlessness, and good judgment. This winning formula will help you deal with the reasons procrastination initially occurs. You will discover that you will start moving things along much sooner and will give yourself more opportunities to choose from.

Why You Must Execute

My most incredible mentors have always told me some version of the following statement, "Results are all that matters." While this is halfway true, I've benefited significantly more from taking it a step further. Thus, the saying is best stated as "Efficient and effective results are all that matters." Indeed, producing results should be your primary focus, but there is a clear difference between "results" and "efficient and effective results." Being efficient means doing things optimally. It is about producing with the least amount of waste. Effectiveness describes the ability to deliver the best results. The addition of efficiency and efficacy takes results to unimaginable levels. Consider the former results statement compared to the latter in the following example. *Two people work toward the same goal simultaneously. While both complete the objective, one does so by staying below budget and producing a much better product in half the time. The other goes over budget, takes twice as long, and creates a standard result.* If you could only choose one, which person would you want in your corner?

This exaggerated example paints a familiar picture that many leaders experience. This is why you must execute above all. By pursuing self-mastery, you will produce efficient and effective results when you become an executor. Executing is not about creating average results but striving to be the best. Those who become high executors gain more income and live better lives because they perform above average each and every day. Through their consistency, it becomes second nature for them to seek and destroy all goals. By creating win streaks, they let their momentum guide them from one achievement to the next, and they understand that the more they can categorize as an objective, the better. Therefore, executing becomes a chase of victories, and by adding more wins to the scoreboard, setbacks have little impact on the overall mission. Wouldn't you like to be in a position where you know you can accomplish anything you attempt? Imagine all the choices and opportunities you could make available to you. This is a powerful position to be in, and guess what? —You are capable of getting there. The main thing stopping you is your level of execution.

Executing is about following all the way through from start to finish. Many individuals face challenges with each stage of execution, as they are unaware of how to be intentional about goal setting and achievement. To help this, I've developed five stages of execution that have become my gold standard: planning, initiating, implementing, testing, and delivering.

Planning: The planning stage of execution is where you must create your roadmap. By working the project backward, you can develop a solid plan from start to finish. This is where you should identify your team and required resources and conduct market research if applicable. You will also want to create your timeline while providing a buffer for unforeseen setbacks or delays at each phase. You must outline potential challenges and obstacles to your plan so you can be prepared to overcome them. It is beneficial to be as detailed as possible and remember to write down or type out each benchmark. This is the most critical step, as it will lay the foundation for the rest of your plan. Spend as much time in this stage as possible without procrastinating. For significant projects, it is also wise to develop a summary to reference to go along with the detailed version of your plan.

Initiating: In the initiating stage, you enter your vehicle and step on the gas. You must build your team and start project discussions with your key players during this stage. It is vital to assign your roles at this time and set the tone for your expectations. This stage begins your journey and should be the point where you discuss the "how." This is the time for you to meet with your team and roundtable all potential barriers you identified during the planning stage. You should also open the discussion for feedback and thoughts about other obstacles. Having a different perspective will help ensure your plan is successful. During this stage, you must also conduct any necessary due diligence not done during your planning stage. Expect this stage to last for a while, depending on the scope of your project. Similar to the planning stage, spend a great deal of time here while avoiding procrastination. It is not the time to speed through your process. The initiating stage prepares you and your team to start the clock.

Implementing: The implementing stage starts your clock. This is the point where you start putting your plan into action. During this stage, speed is required to move the project along. If you devoted significant effort to stages one and two, you should be confident you can follow your steps. Each team member has assigned tasks, so you should schedule routine meetings with them to ensure everyone works promptly. While implementing your plan, you must continue to remain strong and cannot let anyone or anything stop the momentum. Your routine meetings will become your time to address barriers, so ensure they are frequent enough for the scale of the project. Communicating only once a month during this stage is highly frowned upon, as you should also regularly check in with each team member between meetings. While implementing your plan, you must keep track of your benchmarks and remain mindful of your timing. To keep the team motivated, you should also celebrate significant benchmarks throughout your project. Once you have reached all benchmarks on your timeline, you can move to the testing stage.

Testing: The testing stage begins your inspection process. During this time, you must review your deliverables and ensure that you and your team addressed the general mission. You must look back at all benchmarks and ensure everything was completed to your liking. This is the point where you compare the results with the expectations and determine if your overall goal has been met. If tasks were not met or things were not completed to your expectations, you must work on finishing them before you can claim goal achievement. Be mindful that everything may not be perfect at this time. Still, if you are generally satisfied with the overall results, you can move forward while improving the individual tasks. Assuming you are satisfied and depending on your goal, you should plan your delivery. However, if you are entirely unsatisfied with the outcome, you must go back to discover where the project went south and rework your plan from there.

Delivering: The delivering stage is where you claim your victory. Depending on your goal, this is the time for you to make your announcement, bring your product/ service to the market, or celebrate your win with your team. This is the ending stage and the time to see and enjoy your results. In the delivery stage, I spend the time taking a short break so I can soak it all in. By acknowledging your success, you can keep yourself motivated and boost your confidence. This time is critical for your development, so take it as seriously as you took every stage. Some people do not engage in the delivering stage, but it is necessary to help you stay consistent and relevant. There is no point in doing all this work and then going silent when reaching the finish line. Think of your goal achievement as the time to deliver your gift to the world. Be loud and proud about your accomplishments.

Working through the five execution stages will keep you on target for mass achievement. It will guide you through the entire course, from starting a plan to finishing a complete project. Executing is about closing the loop and not simply taking action. This proven model will advance you well beyond your peers because it allows you to be intentional about reaching your goals. While others aimlessly strive to achieve their dreams, you can accomplish more by strategizing and following this path, as it will help you better control your time and resources. Dreams will only become a reality with execution. Therefore, you must execute, above all, to carry your ideas into the physical realm.

Why People Don't Execute

Many people don't execute because they were not adequately taught how. This knowledge gap forces individuals to concentrate only on starting and finishing, ignoring everything that occurs in between. Thus, without experience and proper guidance, the goal becomes cloudy along the way. Imagine jumping in your car and trying to reach an unfamiliar destination without a map. You would need to figure out where to turn and what areas to stay away from and would have no orientation of where you are. Many people feel this way without adequate training in executing. Because being lost is an uncomfortable feeling that most want to avoid, these individuals tend only to pursue familiar territory. Therefore, unless tasked with a typical objective, they take all measures to remain in their comfort zone. They will only choose to engage in similar goals they achieved before, keeping them in the "rat race." If tasked with an unfamiliar goal, these individuals struggle to reach it independently, drop the ball, or give up entirely. A solid way to avoid this mishap is to study the five stages of execution mentioned in the previous section. If you find yourself struggling with execution or want to be a better leader in this aspect, then you must learn and teach others how to break down a goal.

Another common reason people don't execute is

their fear of change. This reason is similar to the previous one in that both offer individuals the opportunity to stay in their comfort zone. However, when people are afraid of change, they intentionally avoid anything that requires it, even if it means suffering and struggling in life. In comparison, the previous group wants to change but lacks the skill and confidence to do so. Hopefully, you are not afraid of change. Perhaps you were, but now that you've made it this far in this book, you should have gained enough knowledge to take a different stance. Nonetheless, as a leader, you must know how to deal with this common reason for non-execution. Fearing change will not let someone take the required action to move their projects along effectively. They will always be internally conflicted with the goal unless they change their mindset. Change is fearful because of past adverse outcomes, low motivation, and lack of relatable examples. There are other reasons, but I find these extremely common. Bypassing this fear is possible through mindfulness exercises and interacting with people who have already achieved the same goals. It requires expanding one's mind to higher possibilities. These individuals can move forward and start taking action by changing this mindset.

Many perfectionists struggle with execution. This group focuses so intensely on getting everything right that it prevents them from taking action. Extreme perfectionists want to come up with the perfect idea and timing and get stuck in the planning stage of execution. These individuals wait for the stars to align before initiating their plan. You must understand that taking action is more important than creating the perfect plan. Spending unnecessary time trying to get everything right while not moving forward is dangerous to your career. Progress is the only motion that matters in your success journey, and you cannot progress without taking one step ahead. Perfectionists believe initiating an imperfect plan is riskier than planning for extended periods. This mindset is far from the truth. Delaying progress by being stuck in the planning stage is a definite way to ensure goal failure. I call this thought process "planning to death" because these individuals kill their progress. There will always be setbacks and unplanned challenges because we cannot see the future. Therefore, it is best to identify potential challenges, plan for unexpected ones, and move ahead. Creating a solid plan is much different than creating a perfect one. A perfect plan does not exist; some strategies are better than others but will still face opposition. Many perfectionists have low confidence and lack the grit to overcome challenges, so they want everything to go perfectly. You must develop a winner's mindset and believe in your abilities to accept that challenges will occur and move on.

How to Become an Executor

Setting goals and executing them is the ultimate key to success. Those who fail to perform will witness their dreams fade away and die and will struggle to live up to their expectations. Goal achievers are the minority, and studies show that 92% of people fail to achieve their goals. The 8% who reach them do so by taking action and executing. Therefore, if you genuinely want to live out your dreams, you must fully embrace executing. You can't expect others to do this for you; it is entirely up to you to put in the effort and make things happen. Since failures make up the majority of society, you have to find the passion within you to become extraordinary. I live by the simple thought that some people want it, and others don't. By choosing to become an executor, I have drastically improved my life and the lives of my family. You can do the same by deciding to do what others won't. Others won't execute; they won't take the time to read this book and apply these winning concepts to their lives. You can choose now to take control of your outcomes by executing. Here are a few more ways to learn how to become an executor.

1. **Start small and then go big**

    a. Learning to execute is another life skill that can improve with practice. As I've experienced more and more success and studied others, I realize the gradual progression that takes place. Most high achievers have accomplished incredible feats by moving the needle further ahead each time they reach a goal. Starting small and then going big will give you the experience and confidence to take on larger objectives. This approach lets you learn much about yourself throughout the process while the risk is lower. You will become more familiar with your planning processes and understand your stressors.

b. Executing small goals first allows you to take more chances. Think of this as the time to practice and gain knowledge before the big game. It makes no sense to start with more than you can handle because the stakes will be higher. You can give yourself the time you need to develop yourself and your team while still making progress. Thus, you must seek opportunities to engage in smaller activities and make this a consistent part of your routine. You will be better prepared and increase your chances of achieving your big goals tenfold.

2. Fully understand what goal achievement rewards you

a. This may seem obvious, but you'd be surprised how many people create goals without fully understanding what it gets them. To become an executor, you must think about everything that pursuing your goals will reward you. Doing so creates value and motivation because you will forgo making excuses, knowing what's on the other side of your success. I personally love doing this because it drives me to work harder and faster to reach my targets. Keeping your eye on the prize will allow your subconscious mind to take over, and you will be less likely to give up when times get tough.

b. Spend the time during your planning stage to write down everything that reaching your objective will contribute to your life. Keep this documented somewhere visible so you and your team can see what you will gain. Don't be oblivious to the outcomes of your achievements, as there will be specific things you may be looking for. Engaging in this process also helps you assess your goals and compare them to others that may be similar. You can discover if one is worth pursuing now versus the other by understanding the rewards beforehand. Always know what your life's pursuits will gain you, and you will execute more often.

3. **Build a strong, diverse team**

a. In Chapter 7, you learned the significance of building a solid, diverse support system and how to do it. Doing so is critical to becoming an executor because the success of your achievements will be as strong as its weakest link. It behooves you to develop your team and ensure each member has the support they need to fulfill their roles. With a solid team in your corner, your success will be unlimited as you will work in harmony and move from task to task. However, if your team is weak, you will reduce your chances of success. As you learned, working with a group can offer speed and momentum. Therefore, you should put forth your best effort to avoid going at things alone to preserve time and increase your accomplishments.

b. Studies show that diverse teams increase production and innovation by 35%. As you recall the information about choosing your *starting five lineup,* this is an effective way of creating an inclusive team. Each person bringing their perspective and unique skills will give you the proper edge as you tackle your challenges. Therefore, by developing good relationships and networking with others, you can focus on building something that will allow the team members to work together towards common goals. You will perform better by doing this.

4. **Embrace discipline**

a. The critical ingredient of execution is discipline. Without it, one will not take the required steps to take action. Taking action does not happen by accident; it is an intentional effort to go from inactivity to activity. Pursuing goals consistently carries a high level of discipline, so you need to embrace it more often. Being disciplined will help you remain focused when temptations distract you from your tasks. The higher your level of discipline, the more you will stay the course and eliminate time-wasters.

b. Nothing will stand in the way of achieving your goals when you add discipline to your lifestyle. You learned specific methods to gain it in the previous chapter in the section about time management. Embracing discipline takes determination, and developing it requires a growth mindset and being habitual. With the proper attitude, you will constantly remind yourself that you have the power to succeed or fail. This reality check will keep you in line and propel you forward. Don't let your lack of discipline be why you don't live out your dreams because you will die with regret. Instead, take accountability, lead by example, and embrace it!

5. **Love your reputation**

a. Self-esteem goes a long way in executing your goals; maintaining a good personal reputation will help you boost it. You will not trust yourself to perform if you don't believe in your abilities. Researchers discovered that 70% of people agreed that confidence contributed to their success. You must firmly believe you are capable of achieving your goals, or you will not reach them. I've learned to fall in love with my reputation, which has served me well. Doing this forces me in the thought process of knowing where I stand based on where I have been.

b. Learning to love your reputation has two perspectives. For those who are already there, it means they love what they have accomplished and know they can attain more through increased action. However, for those who do not love their reputation, it means they have more work to do to live up to their standards. Either way, this technique works because it allows one to look in the mirror and evaluate oneself. You will be more likely to execute by setting and living up to high personal standards.

Early in the chapter, you became familiar with Newton's third law of motion: the law of action and reaction. If you don't apply more force to your goals than the opposition puts on them, your dreams will surely die. Studies show that only 3% of people write down their goals, 14% create unwritten ones, and 83% have none. The 3% of individuals who write down their goals are 30 times more successful than the 83% who don't have them and three times more successful than the 14%

who don't write them down. Therefore, it pays to set goals and take action. The more intentional you become about goal achievement, the better. Don't let anything stop you from executing because it will set you apart and satisfy your desires. I've given you all you need to become an executor. Following this path will lead you to uncharted territory and high achievement. However, if you choose not to execute, you will be executed by all the forces that overpower your production.

10

The Shield of Resilience

Always Expect Setbacks

The path you chose is full of surprises, not all of which will be positive. I know it's unfortunate, but we all wish every day would be smooth sailing in the sunset. Most people desire an opportunity to look into a crystal ball, hoping to see what the future holds, and would love to explore ways to navigate life to avoid struggles. Knowing this is not remotely close to reality, you must learn to expect and deal with setbacks to prevail. Throughout this book, you were introduced to how setbacks impacted your objectives and learned vital ways to manage them while developing limitless capabilities. You also learned how they relate to executing. Now, I want to offer you a deeper explanation of how these challenges will affect you.

Those who don't strive for lofty goals experience fewer setbacks because they face less resistance. It's relatively easy to live a simple life and not get too involved in dream chasing. In fact, most people choose that fate and elect not to travel the road of reaching their full potential. A recent study uncovered an alarming truth that 98% of people fail to live out their dreams. There are many reasons and excuses for this lack of perseverance, but when it's narrowed down, a significant factor is due to low resilience. The vast majority of society does not have the willpower to face adversity. The American

Psychological Association stated, *"Resilience is the process and outcome of successfully adapting to difficult or challenging life experiences, especially through mental, emotional, and behavioral flexibility and adjustment to external and internal demands."* This definition explains that we must adapt and overcome to be resilient. By doing so, one can face the obstacles they will experience, as they are inevitable. The 2% of the population who live out their dreams understand this way of life and, therefore, do everything within their power to fight the battles.

Everyone deals with some level of unique challenges. In my experience, most of my outstanding achievements came alongside many of my most demanding obstacles. Overcoming them defines me, and I always expect storms to come my way. A journey that is all butterflies and flowers does not lead to ultimate prosperity. Hence, your focus should not be to avoid barriers but to learn to recognize and treat them accordingly. Many people take the wrong approach by creating plans to circumvent their threats. Planning this way does not prepare individuals to handle the danger but teaches them to run from it. However, it always catches up and knocks them down when they least expect it. Therefore, to properly face your barriers, you must shift your focus and learn to time them. With your aim at timing your obstacles, you will be better prepared to fight them when they arrive. Becoming successful will come with pain and suffering; for most, it's part of the journey. When the storms come, you have to be willing to dance in the rain, hail, and lightning. Some of the most significant rewards in life accompany pain, stress, frustration, doubt, and discouragement. The more you train yourself to estimate their arrival, the less they will change your momentum, and the more you will advance. You only set yourself up for failure if you don't expect setbacks.

The higher you ascend, the more setbacks will occur because extraordinary achievements require extraordinary output. If being successful came without challenge, everyone would do it, and society would implode because there wouldn't be anything to strive for. So, by a divine design, the world is filled with tests to see how far we are willing to push ourselves. Those who drive themselves the most receive rewards respective to their efforts. This exchange of perseverance and reward is positively correlated, and this relationship is often misunderstood and underestimated. Hence, by accepting this reality, you will be more equipped to unlock its power. Developing resilience will teach you to maintain positive outcomes by conquering your hardships. Hardship has three results: it destroys you, keeps you neutralized, or helps you progress. Your target is the latter. You must treat your hardships as the enemy they are and fight them like your life depends on it. They will sometimes knock you down, but you have to get up and keep going. When you don't let them stand in your way and keep you down, you will evolve by gaining new skills and coping mechanisms. If you anticipate your hardships, the blow will be less overwhelming when these challenges arise. Keeping this mentality is the first step toward developing more resilience.

Donning Your Shield

Being resilient is like carrying an unbreakable shield that allows you to engage in war with any opposition. It is a mandatory attribute for execution, as one must possess this trait to execute at high levels. If execution is the driving force behind progression, then resilience is the mechanism that helps one keep standing when faced with adversity and get back up when they fall, even when they don't want to. Pursuing your goals without this trait is like starting a war without defensive tactics. Creating a battle without a defensive strategy is suicidal and would lead to much bloodshed. However, individuals choose to do it more often than not. Perhaps it's because they haven't correctly learned the connection between resilience and execution. This relationship is more profound than you think. Both attributes drastically impact the other. Execution without resilience allows individuals to go as far as their limits will take them. Thus, when things become too complex, they will discontinue their pursuit. In contrast, being resilient without execution will cause one to remain stagnant. They will not progress because they will only apply defense with no offense. Therefore, you must link the connection and embody both characteristics to live up to your fullest potential.

Have you ever wondered what causes an individual

to keep striving for more, even after reaching high success? When I was younger, I thought the answer was work ethic, and many people I engage with now feel the same. I used to think one could continuously outwork the other, eventually creating separation over time. So, this became my approach for years, and I finally noticed that the gap between my peers was not large enough. That path left me only feeling unfulfilled and exhausted. The more I studied leadership and started applying certain principles to my life, the more I discovered the flaws behind work ethic theories. Work ethic is a tool used to compare one person to another and does not consider internal competition. Where I failed in the past in reaching high success was that I thought I was competing internally but was using a tool to measure my external competition. However, I discovered that the actual internal measurement tool is resilience. Resiliency is the explanation behind why highly successful people keep going. It is a way to look internally and understand one's breaking point. This thought process helps one know how much chaos they can endure. So, when combining it with execution, it is like donning your shield as you enter the battlefield.

Developing your resilience will help you face anything that comes your way. My career pursuit has been filled with tremendous adversity and dark times. I've been knocked down so many times that I have lost count, but I continue to get up and push forward. Sometimes, I stay down longer than I would like, but these are when the threats are more robust. Most of my

'By increasing your resilience, you will gain stability, and things that may affect others drastically will have little impact on you.'

mentors and people I've ascended alongside have similar stories with different struggles. The point is that we all have built a level of resilience that allows us to push through hardships and phenomena. Even discussing these challenges helps to develop more stability, as they become ways of hardening the shield. Now, through years of practice and devotion to my journey, I genuinely believe I can cope with any challenge because my guard is indestructible. It allows me to continue my ambitious path, which I know is not for the faint of heart. As mentioned, I expect and anticipate setbacks even though I know they can destroy me. Keeping this mindset and deliberate reflection on my reactions to attacks puts me in a continuous zone of evolution. I've learned to analyze my situations and grow from my experience of previous episodes. By doing this, I constantly remind myself that I can get through the hardship and have what it takes to win. This positive reinforcement has become one of my most frequently used tools to get me through the storms. While you pursue your course, you will face adversity. The aim is to develop your defensive strategy: to don your shield and continue hardening it over time. You must focus as much on your defense as your offense, and you will be more equipped to pursue loftier goals. Most people haven't learned this technique, and many aren't willing to put in this effort, so you must think differently. That is the difference between how far you will be ready to go and how likely your chances of getting back up will be when knocked down. Your shield should be as strong as your sword, and you will win the war.

Adapt, Survive, and Evolve

You've learned that handling setbacks and overcoming obstacles are crucial to resiliency. But being resilient doesn't limit itself to only learning how to get up when knocked down. There are many times when the challenge is not necessarily an attack or barrier, but it can also be due to an unforeseen change. In the previous chapter, you were introduced to *environmental opposing forces.* The section described how the external environment causes these forces and can also limit execution. Some examples include changes in government regulation, economic changes, and even pandemics, as experienced with COVID-19. Since these forces cannot be controlled, they must be managed. Therefore, to develop high resilience, one must also become adaptable and evolve. Those who ignore environmental changes will be left in the past.

Adapting to new circumstances is a necessity and helps increase your resilience. By adjusting to the new conditions, one can move further in life. This concept of evolution is centuries old and was made famous by Charles Darwin when he coined the term *survival of the fittest.* Under this theory, Darwin explained that creatures who adapt more to their surroundings are the best suited for longevity and survival. In other words, adapting and evolving will allow one to live longer in one's environment, which is the same for your personal goals. If you don't adjust to the new conditions you face when pursuing your dreams, they will become barriers. One of the most famous examples of a lack of adaptation in today's age is the case of Blockbuster. The company operated between 1985 and 2010 and was a global industry giant. At its peak, Blockbuster was valued at $5.9 billion, had over 9,000 stores, and employed over 84,000 people. However, its leaders struggled to evolve and adapt to new customer demands, ultimately causing its demise as Redbox and Netflix entered the industry with more unique products and services. This case is a typical example of why it pays to be adaptable. However, the lack of adaptability is shared daily among many individuals and organizations who eventually meet the same fate unless they change.

If you want to achieve your wildest dreams, you can't sit around and watch the world change around you without keeping up. Becoming a self-master teaches you to avoid this mistake by balancing your proactive and reactive mind states. We all know the world and the things within it will change because some changes are unforeseen. Hence, you must maintain your situational awareness and keep your eyes and ears to the street as much as possible. Whatever environment you're in will be presented with constant change. It's up to you to see the warning signs, no matter how small they seem, and then you can develop a counteractive plan to address them. By increasing your resilience, you will gain stability, and things that may affect others drastically will have little impact on you. Be open-minded to change, and do not stay rigid. I've witnessed far too many leaders slow down progress, hinder production, go out of business, and sabotage their careers due to rigidity. I personally believe in strict structure but fluidity within it to allow for changes to be made when necessary. With this approach, I can run a tight ship that can maneuver and shift direction when the environment demands it. I run businesses this way and apply the same methods to my aspirations. I remain successful by knowing that I cannot control environmental changes but can adapt to and learn from them. It would be best if you approached your journey the same. Deal with your challenges, but also be willing to change your plan when it calls for it. Don't be ignorant of the fact that nothing will remain the same, and you can increase your longevity. Adapt, survive, and evolve.

Why People Have Low Resilience

An inability to handle pressure causes many individuals to lack resilience. Some just aren't good at bearing the weight that massive goals require, which forces them to settle and be less ambitious. Climbing the success ladder is not as simple as just marking tasks off a checklist. Becoming a high achiever takes constant effort, energy, and good planning. While people should expect challenges, they typically don't properly evaluate their plans, and many err on the side of things going according to plan. Thus, they face immense pressure when their plans go off track because they did not build contingencies. As a result of failure from improper planning, these people decide to reduce their goals to avoid heartache. Besides good planning, some practical ways to handle more pressure include delegating, developing more skills, and increasing coping techniques. If this is your concern, each method is beneficial to helping you carry the load and can prevent you from folding under pressure. You can also try this exercise: *Recall one of your highest achievements, and think about how the pressure made you feel as you were knee-deep into it. Now, reflect on what you did to overcome the stress and apply them to your current scenarios.* We often already have the answers to our problems but need to search within. Reflection exercises like these always help me put things into proper perspective and can help you just as well.

People with negative outlooks on life often struggle with finding resilience. Their mindset prevents them from caring deeply about their outcomes. Therefore, they see no value in overcoming obstacles because their goals aren't authentic. These individuals rarely put one hundred percent into their objectives and develop a passive attitude. Being resilient does not align with negative mindsets, so it becomes a formula for disaster. Have you ever tried to discuss vision with someone with this attribute? You'll realize it's like talking to a brick wall. Those who struggle in this area will require much development because it's a chronic condition to execution. It stops one from looking ahead and results in living only in the present. Hence, maintaining optimism is critical for evolution. A generally positive outlook on life can make one more resilient because they will be more engaged in reaching success. Optimism breeds passion, and being passionate about your pursuits will increase your breaking point and harden your shield.

Another common reason people have low resilience is that they lack emotional intelligence. Being emotionally intelligent means that you can control your emotions in troubled times. Those with low emotional intelligence lose grip on their feelings when triggered by specific things, causing a downward spiral. In times of trouble, they tend to act before thinking and cannot gain control unless someone or something intervenes. They react irrationally and let their emotions get the best of them.

This issue is troublesome for goal achievement because it creates a fear of barriers and causes the individual to run instead of fight. As mentioned, resilience is not about running away from your problems but navigating them and finding solutions. You can't face adversity when you're in a losing battle with your emotions. Nonetheless, focusing on stepping back and thinking before acting can increase your emotional intelligence. Improving your critical thinking skills will take you far. It will also help to learn your triggers through exercising your self-awareness so you can know how to conduct yourself. Today's society is highly emotional, but many can circumvent this weakness through recognition and an intentional plan.

How to Gain High Resilience

High resilience offers many benefits, as you've learned throughout this chapter. For most, this characteristic allows them to pursue any goal without much worry that they will reach the finish line. Many attributes contribute to success, but high resilience is one that creates the separation between those who win and those who WIN BIG. These individuals who have it don't let anything stand in their way. They have that dog mentality that allows them to fight back during their most challenging times. You don't need high resilience to succeed; however, you will need it to become one of the 2% of people who live out their dreams. While others struggle to get past life's barriers, you will overcome adversity as you build upon your resilience. Like all other pillars of self-mastery, gaining it can be learned. The following steps are additional ways to develop this trait.

1. **Learn from your mistakes**

   a. Experience is always the best teacher. You recall the importance of taking action from the previous chapter. The same thing applies here; no matter how much you read and gain information, you will only get closer to your goals with work. Your experiences will develop your skills faster because you will move from theory to application. You will make mistakes along the way, but what you do afterward will reveal your true character. Therefore, as you execute your plans, you must analyze and learn from every mistake. Use these moments as opportunities to know what to do differently the next time.

b. Learning from your mistakes helps build your resilience by familiarity. When an obstacle becomes familiar, we are more likely to overcome it because we've lived through it before. Hence, we can develop a new method as we reattempt the objective. If you do not repeat the same mistakes, your chances of moving past the same barriers can drastically increase. There's mixed research in this area, but I can tell you from my experience that I expanded my progress whenever I analyzed my mistakes and learned from them. Sometimes, a new challenge will emerge, but you will be steps closer to your goals.

2. **Set realistic goals**

a. I'm all for dreaming big and being ambitious, but it's essential also to be realistic when setting goals. Setting unrealistic goals will adversely affect you and lower your resilience. Ensure your goals are attainable and you have the resources or a plan to obtain them. Do not go outside the confines of your reach until you have a solid path to get there. I've pursued lofty goals, some of which have been years in the making, but I've learned to break them into manageable chunks. When people set unrealistic goals, they lose their drive because their pursuit isn't real. The first sign of a significant challenge is all it will take for one to give up when the goal is unrealistic.

b. Have you ever tried shooting a target outside your range? This is what it's like when you don't set realistic goals; you completely miss the mark. No one wants to be way off the mark. It can cause anger and depression and destroy your ambition. However, when people know their target is within range, they become more motivated as they move closer. Thus, they will be more willing to face the challenges.

3. Accountability feeds resilience

a. It should go without saying that accountability feeds resilience. However, many people don't make the connection. Those who struggle with accountability will limit their resilience because they will look for excuses when they should hold themselves accountable. Not taking ownership during challenging situations in your life will decrease your perseverance as it does not allow you to see your flaws. You will be more likely to place blame instead of finding solutions during tough times. Therefore, to build resilience, you must accept full responsibility for your impact on objectives.

b. People who take ownership believe it is their duty to overcome barriers. They are more passionate about success and, thus, do not want to fail because failure will be a reflection of them. Highly accountable individuals are less bothered when situations arise that hinder progress, as they commit early on to seeing things through. They understand that failure or success is in their hands. When you focus on building your accountability, it will set the stage for gaining high resilience. Now that you're seeing how it relates to this topic, reference Chapter 5 to explore more ways to improve in this area.

4. Avoid burnout

a. I firmly believe in taking breaks to preserve and increase energy. If burned out, you will not perform at your best, so you must recognize the signs. It is wise to schedule time off from working on your goals periodically. I highly recommend identifying this break time during your planning stage when pursuing lofty goals. Practicing self-awareness can help you learn your limits and stressors and will keep you from burning out. If you are dead tired, you will be useless and can do more damage than good. Your goals are too significant to risk this type of sabotage when it is avoidable with good time management and awareness.

b. Giving yourself time off can increase your resilience because it benefits your mental and physical well-being. Stressful challenges are already built into your pursuits, so there's no reason to add more stress to the circumstances by being burned out. Burnout lowers your resilience and weakens your shield, so when the barriers arrive, they will be more likely to disrupt your plans and knock you down. However, you can maintain high energy levels and boost adrenaline by creating good practices to avoid it. Nonetheless, if you struggle with procrastination, have an accountability partner so it doesn't become an unintended obstacle.

5. Build contingencies

a. Contingency planning allows one to create backup plans for potential threats. This process will help you navigate your challenges and can increase your resilience. A good contingency plan considers "what-if" scenarios and outlines what to do if specific things happen. Engaging in this activity is an excellent way to boost confidence and increase the likelihood of success. You cannot know everything that may occur, but you will be better prepared by thinking through scenarios.

b. Don't always think you need to reinvent the wheel. Members of your support system may have experience in your venture, so they can provide meaningful data as you develop your plans. Don't be afraid to seek advice when it calls for it. A solid contingency plan can be the determining factor in shifting course when you experience roadblocks.

The primary reason to gain high resilience is to possess the tools to manage any opposition. We are capable of more than we think and can control how we respond to times of hardship and change. Throughout this chapter, you discovered the relationship between resilience and goal achievement. You can win the war by being prepared for each battle and having the proper equipment. Nothing should stand in your way or knock you off course when you commit to building your resilience, as this attribute will protect you from all incoming attacks. The reward is there for the taking, so don't let things prevent you from getting everything you deserve and desire. Walk with your head high, and enter your journey with the courage and confidence the shield of resilience will give you!

Conclusion

The Ten Pillars of Self-Mastery provides a direct path toward reaching your highest potential. This philosophy was intended to give you a way to view life through a clear lens and activate your hidden attributes so you can live out your dreams. I aimed to offer you my methods for success and high achievement by challenging you to reflect within and identify what you must do to be extraordinary. As you've learned, success is interpreted differently among individuals, so reaching your preferred level may require unique steps compared to your peers. However, what remains constant is the fact that highly successful people are fully dedicated to their self-development and evolution. Through your pursuit of self-mastery, you will push yourself to unimaginable heights and achieve more than you ever thought possible. In the Digital Age, so much focus has been placed on grabbing our attention and controlling our actions that it's become a fight to commit to what's essential. Therefore, taking back control to make a difference and write our history becomes even more crucial. You can and will be great if you commit to this pursuit.

Now that you're at the end of this book, you've already made a significant accomplishment. Take the time to consider your mind state as you read through your first few sentences and compare it to how you feel now. My guess is that you may have already started making advancements or plan to take immediate action to evolve. As I stated throughout these chapters, you deserve all you desire. However, don't stand in your own way and be the reason you don't live a highly successful life! Ignorance is bliss; now that you have a defined formula, you have no excuse to live average and be mediocre. I've equipped you with details and step-by-step instructions in each chapter to gain the required attributes to become a self-master. Hopefully, you can see how each pillar supports the others and how to apply these principles to meet your specific needs. Doing so will make you more fulfilled and allow you to become the best version of yourself. Your loved ones will thank you, your teammates will notice a positive difference, and you will experience the benefits of your growth.

I gave you this knowledge to offer a thought-provoking experience and a self-mastery program to study and apply. By breaking down self-mastery into these ten pillars, you can reflect on any chapter related to the current attribute you wish to develop. For example, you can dive back into Chapter 4 and narrow your focus to advance your fearlessness. If you want to become better at manifestation and gaining mindfulness, Chapter 5 will help you get there. These lessons aim to teach you self-mastery as a whole by feeding you the most impactful characteristics in bite-sized pieces you can swallow. Therefore, reading this book should not be a one-time thing but should become a part of your personal leadership development and toolkit. If you have a team, consider sharing this with your members, as it will enhance the performance and productivity of those who commit to their development. Passing this knowledge along can serve as a way for you to give back to society by expanding the minds of those who desire to gain more knowledge and become change agents. Our generational evolution depends on those willing to be highly successful and more influential than their predecessors. However, it requires the dedication you have displayed by getting here and taking your time to reach this final moment in *Achieving SELF-MASTERY in the Digital Age.* Recite and remember the following acronym.

Situational, Exemplary, Limitless, Fearless,

Mindful, Accountable, Supporting, Timely,

Executor, Resilient

SELF-MASTER

About the Author

Marco McKithen is a business operations expert and high achiever who has led many groups, teams, and organizations throughout his career. Growing up in Buffalo, NY, he knows what it takes to come from poverty and challenging environmental conditions to live a life filled with opportunities, freedom, and success. While still evolving, Marco has faced extreme adversity, some of which include homelessness, racism, and undesirable challenges as a young father in the lower class. He now controls his own destiny and works every day doing what he loves—helping improve the lives of many as a healthcare administrator and business owner. The author embodies exemplary leadership and lives by the philosophies he presented throughout this book. While serving in the US Navy, he received many accolades, including two Navy and Marine Corps Achievement Medals, multiple letters of commendation, and Blue Jacket of the Year, 2018, a high unit achievement. Marco is a firm leader with high expectations of his followers, not only because he wants to bring out the best in them but because he has high expectations of himself and loves to win. He is described by many as "someone who makes everyone better around him." He genuinely believes that everyone has an opportunity of choice, and they can choose how they approach life. This mentality has led him here to write this book and provide the keys to his ambition and wisdom behind his unlimited evolution.

The author attributes his life's success to the confidence instilled in him by his single mother at an early age. She always taught him that becoming great required thinking big; by doing so, he learned he would not be limited to his surroundings, only his thoughts. Unlike many young peers, he took his mother's teachings to heart and developed a creative mind, becoming an artist and entering art school around age six. He would continue his path as an artist throughout his senior year of high school. Art became Marco's way of dreaming and allowed him to research and explore the world from a different perspective. It continued to raise his curiosity and helped develop his growth mindset. He explains now that most of his innovation in business is derived from his artistic mind because he can visualize every idea he thinks about. He is a true visionary, which allows him to be an extraordinary strategist. The positive affirmations from his mother and the opportunity she gave him to be limitless all contribute to his success as a business leader.

Fast forward to adulthood, Mr. McKithen had his first child at age twenty-one. He was not financially or mentally prepared to be a father and had lost his way after high school. Marco did not stick with the path he had set. He allowed his environment to hinder his progress and cloud his judgment, and he started letting life's challenges bring him down. Therefore, he struggled for years to come after having his daughter. With a second child, the author reinvented himself at twenty-four when he joined the US Navy. He knew he needed a drastic change to get back on track and reshape his mind, and the military became his outlet. He joined the reserves and started attending college in 2011, and it became the most pivotal point in his life. Marco's military experience gave him a new hope in life, awakening the same mind state he had as a child— the belief that dreaming big creates unlimited opportunity. Marco began his leadership journey with his newfound environment and support system, becoming a leader in his reserve military unit and civilian job. He spent years in the account receivables industry, working his way up from supervisor, manager, and eventually, co-owner of his firm. This experience gave him strategic planning, operations, and business development skills as a leader in a challenging industry. Around the same time, he started a new relationship with the person who would become the love of his life and now fiancé. He soon after had his third child and desired to become the best role model he could be to his expanded family. So, he focused on setting his new life plan and stuck to it.

Marco continued to thrive as a business owner and relocated to Florida in 2016 after lengthy discussions with one of his closest friends/business partners. Mr. McKithen's goal was to change his environment for better opportunities and outcomes, and he realized that moving was his best chance. While there, Marco also continued his education, graduating with his Bachelor of Science in Health Services Administration in 2019. However, he did not want to stop there, so he began working towards his Master's degree, graduating in 2021 with a Master's of Business Administration in Complex Health Systems. While pursuing his education, Marco opened his own company, Systematic Developers Inc., a business management and consulting firm. Through there, he helped small business owners with business strategy, coaching, and leadership development. Marco worked with many entrepreneurs, increased profits, and helped them expand. He also became a healthcare administrator during this era, aligning with his personal goals and dreams. He is now an Army Officer Candidate in the Kansas National Guard and plans to attend law school to become an attorney. Mr. McKithen continues living out his dreams and pushing the bar higher with each achievement and does not plan to stop anytime soon.

Marco McKithen wrote this book to spread this knowledge and lead the path for those who want to achieve more. He believes that society needs it now more than ever before and that, somehow, people have lost their way. Therefore, Marco wants to spark the minds of others who may not have the proper guidance but want a better lifestyle. His perspective gives him an advantage: he notices the signs of an adverse society. However, the author genuinely thinks that one person at a time can create positive change, and he works hard to become a mentor and share his wealth of knowledge with others. Marco wants to help develop more effective leaders by sharing his life experiences and path to success. He aims to show that if someone from his background can live prosperously, many others can do the same. Mr. McKithen has learned that leading others effectively is possible by leading oneself and evolving above all.

* 9 7 9 8 2 1 5 0 3 3 1 5 9 *